Poetry and Underwear
and Other Stories

By Ole Giese

To: Gwen!
Hope you enjoy this read!
[signature]

OG Creations
Greensboro

Published by
OG Creations
607 Woodland Drive
Greensboro, NC 27408
www.olegiese.com

LCCN: 2012903252
ISBN: 978-0-9851852-1-3

Available at:
www.olegiese.com

Printed in the United States of America

"A wild improbable treasure hunt in Russia, a kidnapping of a bicycle with political implications, and a determined cleaning woman putting up with an anti-establishment poet . . ."
Jane D'Auvray, Magazine Marketing Director

"Most entertaining . . . author's observations of human motivation and quest, laced with humor make for enjoyable reading."
Donald Smith M.D.

To my grandchildren, Sarah, Caroline, Liza and Caitlyn.

Acknowledgements

Thank you to friends of mine who read the manuscripts. My sincere thanks for their encouragement. Without their enthusiasm, this book would not have been published.

Yolanda M. Johnson-Bryant, literary consultant, who edited this book and helped me navigate the publishing "jungle", Peg Robarchek, for the copyediting. And, to Tami Topalu, artist, who designed the book cover.

POETRY AND UNDERWEAR
AND OTHER STORIES

POETRY AND UNDERWEAR
AND OTHER STORIES

Salad Dressing

Athena's Disciples

Poetry and Underwear

OLE GIESE

OLE GIESE

SALAD DRESSING

Chapter 1

Jerry Sweikert approached the desk clerk in his Moscow hotel. "Can you suggest a good restaurant; a place serving typical Russian food—reasonably priced—like some sort of family restaurant?"

"Certainly," answered the clerk, with a big smile. "One of the most sought after places to eat in Moscow is Restaurant Borovsky. It's located near Kremlin Square. I'll show you the location on this map. It's easy to find and not far from here—only a ten minutes walk."

Jerry had arrived that morning from the United States, part of a tourist group from Cincinnati. His fellow tourists were about to board a sightseeing bus for a tour of the city and visits to museums and art galleries. Jerry remained in the lobby. He was tired from the overseas flight and needed to get a shower *and* some rest.

The tour guide, seeing him standing away from the group, approached him. "Mr. Sweikert, are you not coming along?" she asked.

"No, I'm worn out and need to freshen up and get a nap. I'm not very interested in visiting museums and the like. I prefer exploring the city on my own."

Jerry, a bachelor in his early thirties, was the owner and chef of a well-known restaurant in Cincinnati. The most popular items on his menu were a large selection of salad dishes. Whenever Jerry traveled, he was always on the lookout for new dishes to expand his menu.

With map in hand, he navigated a maze of streets and squares before arriving at Restaurant Borovsky. It was a large place. The walls were painted in various shades of red and covered with paintings of Russian landscapes. A large picture of Lenin hung on one of the walls. The tables were covered with red and white checkered tablecloths.

A distinct smell of food filled the room and the restaurant was full of guests. Waiters dressed in black and large white aprons scuttled between tables taking orders and delivering a steady stream of dishes.

Jerry sat down at the only table available and ordered a vodka. The maitre d' handed him an English menu. Jerry studied it and noticed a large variety of salads. He was not very hungry, so he selected soup, borscht, and a salad.

He called a waiter to his table. "Your selection of salads is very large. What would you recommend?"

"*Salad a la Kremlin*," the waiter suggested.

After Jerry finished his soup, he dug into the salad and was amazed. It was delicious and the salad dressing was incredibly tasty. When he had finished eating, he waived the waiter over.

"Do you speak English?" he asked.

"A little," the waiter answered.

"The salad was out of this world. Do you know what the ingredients are in the dressing?"

"I not quite understand, Sir," the waiter responded in broken English.

"I mean, how is the salad sauce made? What's in it?"

"I not know. I'm not a cook. I think it's oil, vinegar, and other things."

Jerry paused for a moment. "Could you call the owner or chef so I can talk to him?"

"Mr. Borovsky is very busy in kitchen. He tell us not disturb him," the waiter replied.

Jerry became increasingly impatient. "Go get him anyway!" he demanded.

The waiter reluctantly headed for the kitchen. A few minutes later Borovsky appeared. He was a heavy-set burly man. A large apron wrapped around his massive waist showed traces of his profession. The waiter followed at a respectful distance as Borovsky approached Jerry's table . . . visibly irritated.

"What do you want?" Borovsky asked.

"Mr. Borovsky, your *Salad a la Kremlin* is terrific. The taste is great! My name is Jerry Sweikert, here's my card. I own a restaurant in America. One of my most popular dishes is a house salad that has been praised in several gourmet magazines. I would really like to get the recipe for *your* salad dressing, and in return I will give you mine."

"No!" Borovsky exclaimed. "I don't give out my recipe to *anyone*. It's a family secret handed down to me by my grandmother. And I'm not interested in *your* recipe either." With that, Borovsky abruptly returned to the kitchen and the waiter handed Jerry his check.

Back at the hotel, Jerry reflected on his unpleasant encounter with Borovsky. As he slumped on the bed in his room, the thought of getting hold of Borovsky's recipe obsessed him.

How can I get my hands on that recipe? He asked himself repeatedly.

Suddenly, he sat up on the bed. "I've got it! It's simple. I'll take a small sample and have it analyzed," he said aloud.

Chapter 2

The next day, around noon, Jerry returned to Borovsky's restaurant with a small plastic container in his pocket. When he arrived, the server who waited on him the day before saw him and disappeared into another part of the restaurant. Another waiter approached Jerry's table. Jerry simply pointed at the *Salad a la Kremlin* on the menu.

"Anything else?" the waiter asked.

"Yes, a vodka please."

"No more food?" the waiter inquired.

"No, the salad is enough."

The salad arrived and Jerry started eating. He looked around in the restaurant to make sure no one was looking. He carefully scooped a small amount of the dressing and poured it into the plastic container. He finished the salad, paid the check and left the restaurant.

Upon Jerry's return to the hotel, the travel group was ready to leave Moscow for St. Petersburg. Jerry, anxious to get home quickly, told the tour guide, "I must take care of some things back home, so I'm bailing out".

Surprised, the tour guide said, "I'm sorry to hear that. You have only been here a few days. You will miss the trip to St. Petersburg. It's a very interesting city—full of exciting sights, a famous art museum, and the Palaces of the Tsars."

"I know, but I absolutely need to get back home to deal with a few important matters which need my attention."

Jerry shook hands with the tour guide and hurried back to his room to pack. He wrapped the sample of salad dressing in some dirty underwear and closed his suitcase. Early the next morning he booked an afternoon flight to Cincinnati.

- - - -

As Jerry was passing through U.S. Customs, he was stopped by an official. "Have you anything to declare?" the official asked, "Or, do you carry any foodstuffs of any kind from abroad?"

"Nothing," Jerry replied.

"Please open your suitcase," the customs official instructed.

The official searched the contents of Jerry's luggage, moving his hands around in the suitcase. He found the small plastic container. Holding it high, he asked, "What is this?"

"I suffer from chronic constipation. I need to take it to alleviate the symptoms," Jerry responded.

The customs official opened the lid, sniffed the content and said, "Boy, it smells good. What a wonderful aroma."

"Yes, it's great when an effective remedy has a pleasant smell."

That was a close call, Jerry thought, once outside the airport. He hailed a taxi and went home.

Chapter 3

The next morning, Jerry feverishly flipped through the pages in the telephone book to locate a laboratory. He decided on one called Nutritional Labs Inc., and phoned for an appointment. A receptionist answered his call.

"My name is Jerry Sweikert. I have something that needs to be analyzed. Can I talk to the head of your lab?"

"Let me talk to our director," the receptionist said. "Hold on."

A few minutes later, the director came on the line. "What do you want to have analyzed Mr. Sweikert?" he asked.

"A salad dressing."

"A *salad* dressing? Why?"

"It was in a salad I had during a recent visit to Moscow. I need to know the ingredients of the dressing, and its ratios."

"I don't quite understand. Everybody knows that a salad dressing contains oil, vinegar and a few spices!"

"True, but this is a unique dressing," Jerry answered.

"Mr. Sweikert, we are up to our eyeballs in work right now. All my staff is involved in a crucial analysis of hamburger meat. A woman claims she got food poisoning from eating a burger in a diner here in Cincinnati. I believe the place is called Chez Jerry."

Jerry was perplexed. *Shit! Now I'm facing a goddamned lawsuit, and this fellow has the audacity to call my restaurant a diner.*

"Mr. Sweikert, I'll phone you in a few days when we are less busy," the director said, breaking Jerry's thoughts.

The risk of a lawsuit and the inability to have the sample analyzed quickly were complications that ate at him. Anxious to know the result of the analysis of the meat, Jerry phoned the lab director a couple of days later and said, "I contacted you a few days ago about an analysis of a salad dressing sample."

"Oh yes, I remember."

"Last time I talked with you, you also mentioned something about an analysis of some hamburger meat."

"Mr. Sweikert, why are you interested in the analysis of the meat?" the director asked.

"The woman ate the hamburger in *my* restaurant. Do you have the results?"

"We have not yet completed the analysis. But, we are close, and I can now allocate my staff to analyze your salad dressing sample. Bring it to us on Monday of next week."

- - - -

On the day of the appointment, Jerry took the sample to the lab. He met with the director, who opened it.

"Do you mind if I smell it?" the director asked.

"No, go right ahead," Jerry obliged.

"Wow, what an aroma. We'll have the analysis of the salad dressing ready for you in a week or so."

While awaiting the result of the analysis, Jerry's mind was totally preoccupied by the Russian salad dressing—so much that one night he had a dream about it.

Elegantly dressed in a business suit, he was sitting in a richly appointed office suite. From there he could see down below, a factory floor that was buzzing with workers producing salad dressing. Long lines of filling stations were operating around the clock. Workers in the shipping department were moving crates of bottled salad dressing into a stream of waiting trucks for nationwide distribution. The dressing had become a huge success.

He saw throngs of eager shoppers pushing and shoving to get into supermarkets where shelves were stocked inches deep with *Jerry's Salad Dressing*.

- - - -

He woke up, dizzy from his dream, slid into his slippers and stumbled out to the bathroom. He looked in the mirror above the vanity. His hair was in a mess and the underwear he slept in was wrinkled and out of place.

With a deep sigh, he mumbled to himself, "Blasted salad dressing."

13

- - - -

Finally the director of Nutritional Labs Inc., phoned him. "We have completed the analysis of the salad dressing. It shows the following standard ingredients: olive oil, balsamic vinegar, mustard, some dashes of Tabasco and honey."

"Anything else?" Jerry asked.

"Yes. There are tiny traces of something else, but we have not been able to identify it because the sample is so small. Maybe it's a Russian herb unfamiliar to me."

"What about the ratios?"

"We could only determine very approximate ratios. To do a more exact analysis, we would need a much bigger sample. You see, in a mixed fluid, the ratio determination depends on which part of the mixture the sample is drawn from. Is there anything else we can do for you?"

"No, I guess that's all."

"All right then, we'll send you the analysis *and* our bill tomorrow," the director said before hanging up the phone.

Faced with the risk of a lawsuit due to the possibility of tainted meat at his restaurant, and the inconclusive outcome of the salad dressing analysis, Jerry fell into despondency. He lost his appetite and got very little sleep, as he dragged himself through each day. His interest in his restaurant declined and the supervision of his personnel became slack. They noticed that something was wrong with the boss.

Jerry made an appointment with his physician. Sitting nervously in the waiting room, he reached for one of the magazines that were neatly arranged on a side table. His eyes fell on *Today's Gourmet*. He opened it, glanced at a few pages and then absentmindedly tossed it back in the pile.

A nurse appeared. "Mr. Sweikert, the doctor can see you now."

Jerry followed her into the physician's office.

"Hi, Jerry, you look pale. What's the problem?" the doctor asked.

"A salad dressing *and* a possible lawsuit", Jerry mumbled.

"What? A salad dressing?" the doctor exclaimed. "That's a first in my thirty five years of practicing medicine. Tell me about it *and* the lawsuit."

"Well, I had a wonderful salad dish during my recent trip to Moscow. I asked the restaurant owner for the salad dressing recipe. He refused and it's driving me nuts. On top of this, I'm at risk for a possible lawsuit. Some woman who had a hamburger in my place claims she got food poisoning."

"I see," the doctor said as he jotted something down on a notepad. "Here is a prescription for Valium. This will calm you down and hopefully you'll feel better."

- - - -

Increasingly worried about the analysis of the meat, Jerry phoned the lab again and got the director on the line.

"Last time I talked with you," Jerry said, "you mentioned that the analysis of the meat was close to completion. Is there any news?"

"Yes. There was no problem with the meat. It turned out to be fine. As you know, a lot of people try to make a buck on bogus claims. Crap like that comes our way all the time. It's a disgrace. The woman probably had a pre-existing intestinal condition."

With the potential meat problem resolved, Jerry felt better. In time, he overcame his depression. However, the Russian salad dressing kept popping up in his thoughts. For weeks, he tried to forget it, but it kept lurking in his mind. Although he'd already been through a lot of trouble to get his hands on the recipe, he decided to return to Moscow. He felt he had to take a final stab at getting the recipe.

There has to be another way to get my hands on that recipe, Jerry thought.

Chapter 4

Upon his return to Moscow, Jerry checked into the same hotel as before. The clerk at the reception desk recognized him.

"Welcome back to our hotel, Mr. Sweikert. Nice to see you again. I can well understand why you like our city. It has so many interesting attractions to explore."

"I know, but the purpose of my return is something else, and I wonder if you can help me."

"I'll try," the clerk answered. "How can I assist you?"

"Some month ago, during my first visit to Moscow, I had lunch at Restaurant Borovsky.

"Was the meal good?"

"Yes, delicious! *Especially* the *Salad a la Kremlin*. The dressing was very tasty. I tried to get the recipe from Mr. Borovsky, but he refused to give it to me. He said it was a family secret. I wonder if there is another way to get it."

The clerk waived Jerry closer to the counter, leaned over and whispered, "The Mafia." In a low voice, he continued, "They are in the telephone book. But to make it easy for you, here is some information that may interest you."

The clerk retrieved a colorful brochure from a desk drawer. The name of the organization was *OMNIA*. Jerry read the pamphlet:

Sanitation – Transportation – Hospitality – Surveillance – Consulting - Mediation – Public Relations – Sundry Services

"I'm certain they can assist you," the clerk continued. "Their telephone number is in the brochure, which by the way, is only given out in special cases. So please keep this information between you and me, and do *not* share it with anyone."

"These Russians are weird," Jerry said to himself, once he was back in his room. "The clerk told me to keep this matter a secret. Yet, he gave me a printed pamphlet."

Jerry sat down on the bed. He thought it would be unusual and dramatic to enlist the Russian mob's help to get the recipe. But, then again, if that is what it would take, why not?

He dialed the number in the pamphlet that the clerk had given him. A telephone operator answered.

"OMNIA, Sonia speaking. How can we be of assistance?"

"My name is Jerry Sweikert. I'm a visitor from the United States and I would like to have an appointment with the boss of your organization."

"You mean, the president of our company?"

"Oh, I'm sorry, madam, I misspoke."

"Just a moment, Sir, I'll switch you over to his private secretary. Hold on." Jerry heard the sounds of *Tchaikovsky's Piano Concert No.1* while he waited.

The secretary came back on the line. "Mr. Sweikert, what *exactly* is it that you'd like to meet with our president about?"

"It's about a private matter," Jerry answered, not wanting to reveal too much information.

- - - -

The secretary entered the president's office, told him that an American gentleman was on the phone, and wanted an appointment with him.

"What does he want?" the president asked.

"The gentleman said it's a private matter."

"An American wants to see me about a private matter? Couldn't he be a bit more specific? Doesn't he know that we have an affiliate in New Jersey? Why didn't he contact them? But, hell, since he *is* in Moscow, schedule him for Monday of next week at 3:00 p.m. Maybe it's something big. And, by the way, send one of our limousines to pick him up and give him the code word: *Dove*."

The secretary relayed the information to Jerry.

"By the way, what is the name of the president of your company?" Jerry asked.

"Sorry, it's our corporate policy not to give out individual names by telephone."

- - - -

While waiting for his appointment with OMNIA, Jerry seldom left the hotel. When not eating in the dining room and downing vodka after vodka in the bar, he remained in his room playing Solitaire, watching BBC news, and reruns of American movies on television.

- - - -

One evening, after dinner, Jerry sat at the bar. A middle-aged couple sat down next to him. The man was tall and beefy and wore checkered shorts. He had on long white socks and sneakers. His bulging chest and belly were covered by a red t-shirt, indicating that he was a customer of *Jimmy's Hardware*. An old-fashioned camera dangled around his neck and a baseball cap featuring *Ollie's Feeds* rounded off his outfit.

His wife, a small woman, wore jeans with sequins along the seams, a white t-shirt with *I Love Utah* on it, and a pair of high top canvas sneakers. The man downed a couple of vodkas as his wife sipped Coca-Cola. He turned toward Jerry.

"Howdy. Are you American?" he asked.

"Yes I am," Jerry answered.

"I'm Oscar and my lady here is Mary Lou. We hail from Utah. I own a thousand acre farm—had cattle before, but now I grow corn. It's a bonanza, you know, with all that corn they put in the gas nowadays. So, the kitty is plenty full. It's a lot more profitable than screwing around with a bunch of dumb cattle. So why not shell out some dough and see the world? That's why we're here."

"I see," Jerry uttered.

Oscar continued, "Are there any interesting things to see here in Moscow? I mean tourist attractions and the like . . . and, of course, some decent chow?"

"I guess so," was Jerry's response.

"What do you mean? Haven't you seen anything of interest here?"

"Not really. I'm here on business."

"What is your business?" Oscar inquired.

"I own a restaurant in Cincinnati."

After a moment of reflection, Oscar continued, "I've got it. You are here to scout for Russian grub."

"Sort of," Jerry responded.

"Speaking of food, do you happen to know a restaurant here in Moscow that you can recommend?"

"Yes, Restaurant Borovsky. I've been there twice. You have to try their *Salad a la Kremlin*. It's excellent."

"Do we have to dress up?"

"Oh, no! You can go as you are. It's neither a highbrow restaurant nor a pricey one. It's a family-style place."

"Great!" Oscar exclaimed. He turned toward Mary Lou and said, "Let's have lunch there tomorrow. Is that okay with you, Sweetie?"

"Yes, Honey," she said as she took a sip of her Coke.

Chapter 5

The following afternoon, Jerry paced the reception area anxiously awaiting the return of the Utah couple. He was interested in knowing what they thought of the salad dish. When they turned up, Jerry approached Oscar.

"How was your lunch?" Jerry asked them. "Did you try *Salad a la Kremlin?*"

"Yes, unfortunately," Oscar sighed. "It was awful! We didn't like it at all. The dressing was far too spicy and gooey. Mary Lou now has an upset stomach. Look at her. She's all pale. No doubt because of that shitty salad dressing!"

"I don't understand," Jerry countered. "It's one of their most popular dishes—a specialty of the house."

"I don't care," retorted Oscar. "Our lunch was a total disaster. The rest of the day is shot and Mary Lou has to lie down now. What a mess!"

"I make a much more tasty salad dressing," Mary Lou added in a feeble voice. "My Uncle Emil gave me the recipe. He was a cook in a joint in a small town in Utah. I think it was called *Bubba's Place*. If you want it, I can give you the recipe."

Jerry rolled his eyes looking up at the ceiling. He had no interest in Uncle Emil's dressing.

"Do you want the recipe?" Mary Lou insisted.

"Yes, I may be interested," Jerry obliged.

Mary Lou noticed Jerry's lack of interest and stared at him with disdain. Turning toward her husband she said, "Come Oscar, let's get up to our room." In a huff, she headed for the elevator with Oscar in tow.

Jerry slumped into a chair in the reception area. He didn't understand. The customs official and the lab fellow both loved the aroma of the dressing. And here were some peasants, right out of the cornfields, talking it down.

Maybe palates in Utah are not sophisticated enough to appreciate a delicacy, he thought.

- - - -

On the day of his meeting with the chief of OMNIA, Jerry walked around aimlessly in the hotel lobby. He had put on his best suit—a dark one, a dark blue shirt and black necktie. He cleaned a pair of dark sunglasses with a Kleenex and put them on.

The limousine driver, dressed in black and wearing dark glasses, entered the hotel through the large rotating glass door. He approached Jerry and asked, "Are you Mr. Sweikert?"

"Yes I am."

"What is your code word?"

"Dove," Jerry replied.

"Just a moment, Sir," the driver said as he headed for the reception desk.

The clerk handed the driver a bundle of cash, which he put in an attaché case.

"Okay Mr. Sweikert, we are ready to roll."

Jerry noticed that part of a shoulder holster and a revolver handle were visible under the driver's jacket. He led Jerry to a black stretch limousine parked outside and opened the door. Jerry settled into the comfortable backseat. The interior was equipped with a pullout bar that housed a selection of liquors, an ice bucket and glasses. Inside the limo were two telephones and the car's tinted windows were thick. Jerry was a little on edge, so he fixed himself a vodka to calm his nerves.

The car moved rapidly through the streets, ignoring the speed limit and several red lights. It finally came to a stop in front of the gated entrance to the headquarters of OMNIA. At the end of the long driveway was a modern and massive multi-story building, surrounded by a large manicured lawn dotted with neatly arranged flowerbeds. A fleet of black limousines was parked in a huge lot next to the building. The driver picked up his phone and the heavy iron gate opened.

Jerry followed the driver into a large lobby. He was checked in at the reception desk and passed through a metal detector. After being frisked, he was given a nametag. Men and women, all dressed in black, scurried through the myriad of corridors carrying briefcases and reams of paper. Jerry was led through three heavy glass doors guarded by men in dark suits, before arriving at the front office of the president of

OMNIA. He was searched again as he checked in at yet another reception desk. He was directed to sit in an elegantly appointed waiting room. Antique paintings covered the walls and large ornate vases held colorful flower arrangements.

A few moments later, a man who Jerry assumed was a waiter emerged. "Sir, would you like a refreshment?"

"Yes. A vodka, please."

The waiter brought the drink and Jerry drank it in one gulp.

Ten minutes and another vodka later, a secretary appeared. Jerry was steered through two armored doors, into the private office of the president.

The president rose from his ornate painted desk when Jerry entered. Behind the desk hung a large full-size painting of him in shirtsleeves and a shoulder holster that held a gun. The two men shook hands.

"I'm Lamansky, nice to meet you Mr. Sweikert. Let's sit down over here. It's more comfortable." The men settled into deep leather chairs.

"I admire your beautiful desk," Jerry said.

"Yes, it's nice. It's an eighteenth century Italian piece—a gift from a colleague in Sicily. We've had a very productive business relationship for years," Lamansky explained. "Well, Mr. Sweikert, would you care for a drink?"

Jerry really wanted another vodka, but seeing a half-empty bottle of Perrier on Lamansky's desk, he felt it would be tactful to have a Perrier as well.

"A Perrier please."

Lamansky rang a bell on his desk and a waiter emerged. "Two Perriers. Make it snappy! We are both *very* thirsty."

"Yes Sir!" the waiter replied.

"What can I do for you Mr. Sweikert?" Lamansky asked, turning his attention to Jerry.

"Call me Jerry," he replied.

The invitation to informality was ignored by Lamansky. Jerry took note and continued. "Let me explain. Some months ago, I had lunch at Restaurant Borovsky. I had a wonderful salad there. The dressing was terrific—a wonderful taste."

"I know the place," Lamansky injected. "Go on."

"I asked Mr. Borovsky for the recipe for the salad dressing, but he refused. This is why I'm here. You see, I own a restaurant in the United States. That's why I'm interested in getting the recipe."

"What!" Mr. Lamansky exclaimed. "You're here to see me about a salad dressing?"

"Yes, Mr. Lamansky. I understand your organization may be able to help me get the recipe," Jerry explained.

Lamansky became visibly irritated. "Mr. Sweikert, our company works on large diversified projects. It is rather ridiculous to bother my organization with such an unimportant matter!"

Lamansky paused for a moment and continued. "On the other hand, this may be an assignment for one of our young trainees. You see, Mr. Sweikert, we are constantly recruiting young men and women so that our company can continue to grow and expand. The retirement age in this organization is sixty-five, and we need continuous infusions of new blood."

He got up and called his secretary. "Get me the list of our trainees!"

Minutes later Lamansky's secretary handed him a leather file. He studied the list inside and turned toward the secretary.

"The evaluation of this fellow, Igor, is very good. Ask personnel to send him to my office right away!"

A few, short moments later, Igor entered Lamansky's office.

He's just a kid, Jerry thought. *Barely twenty years old.*

Standing ramrod straight, Igor addressed Lamansky. "Sir, you sent for me?"

"Igor, do you like salad?"

Igor hesitated.

Lamansky raised his voice, "Spit it out!"

"Well Sir, it's not my favorite dish."

"It's very good for you—it's healthy."

"Yes, Sir, it is."

"Igor, Mr. Sweikert here needs to get hold of a salad dressing recipe from Restaurant Borovsky. It's your job to get it. Remember the training you've received from this organization and use your own imagination in accomplishing this task. Talk to your instructor first. He will give you some advice on how to go about it. The audience is over. You can leave now."

Igor bowed toward the gentlemen and left the office.

23

Lamansky turned toward Jerry and said, "As you can probably understand, our enterprise is not a charitable one. We are compensated for our services."

"Of course, I understand," Jerry answered.

"Mr. Sweikert, we have a certain charge for specific assignments. This salad dressing job is a small project and it falls under our miscellaneous category. We will agree to take on this small job for one thousand dollars plus expenses."

"What expenses would be associated with this assignment?" Jerry asked.

Lamansky smiled. "Igor's meal at Borovsky's restaurant, plus tips. Young people like Igor usually have huge appetites, so he will probably order a three course lunch or dinner."

"I understand. Can I pay for your services by credit card?"

"No, we only take cash!"

"I don't have that much on me now," Jerry ventured.

"No problem," Lamansky answered. "When you get back to your hotel, just give the money to the clerk at the reception desk. You see Mr. Sweikert, we operate on trust." He chuckled. "We have, of course, means to ensure that trust. To simplify things, Igor's meal expenses will be added to your tab at your hotel, which happens to be owned by this organization."

The two men shook hands and Jerry left Lamansky's office. A limousine took him back to his hotel. Once they arrived, the driver followed him to the reception desk. When the clerk handed Jerry the key to his room the driver said, "I was told a payment is due."

"Oh yes," Jerry said, "I will be back in a minute."

A few moments later, he returned with a wad of bills, and he handed it over to the hotel clerk. After having carefully counted the money, the clerk put it in a safe.

"Can I get a receipt?" Jerry asked the clerk.

The driver said, "Sir, we don't issue receipts."

- - - -

That evening, Jerry went down to the restaurant area and took his usual seat at the bar.

The bartender greeted him. "Have you had a good day here in Moscow?"

"Yes, very productive. Give me a vodka."

Chapter 6

A few days later, around noon, a black limousine pulled up in front of Borovsky's restaurant. The owner, who happened to be in the dining room, noticed the vehicle.

He turned to the maitre d' and said, "I see we are going to have some distinguished guests." He called one of his waiters and told him and the maitre d', "Remember to give these important people tip-top efficient service. Nothing must go wrong. Do you understand?"

"Yes, Mr. Borovsky," they answered in unison.

The driver opened the passenger door. Igor stepped out and entered the restaurant. Once inside, he adjusted his necktie and dark glasses.

Borovsky greeted him. "Welcome, Sir, to my restaurant. Where would you like to sit?"

"Over by the window," Igor replied in a nonchalant tone.

"Sir, a waiter will be with you right away." Borovsky bowed and left for the kitchen.

Shortly after, a waiter appeared.

"Would you care for a drink?" he asked.

Without looking up, Igor replied, "A Perrier."

Igor drank it quickly and waived the waiter back to his table. "Another one," he instructed.

The waiter did what he was told and brought Igor another Perrier and a menu. Igor hardly looked at it before ordering *Salad a la Kremlin* and pepper steak.

"Thank you, Sir," the waiter said, taking Igor's menu. He left for the kitchen to give Borovsky the order.

"Did you ask the guest if he wants his steak well-done, medium or rare?" Borovsky asked.

"No I forgot."

"For heaven's sake go and find out! What did I tell you a moment ago about efficient service?" Borovsky snapped.

The waiter returned to Igor's table and asked the crucial question.

"I don't care," Igor replied. "Leave it to the cook."

Bewildered, the waiter went back to the kitchen.

26

"So, how does he want it cooked?" asked Borovsky.

"He said to leave it to the cook."

Clearly irritated, Borovsky mumbled, "That young fellow can't be very sophisticated. He doesn't even know what he wants. I'll make it rare."

Igor started eating the salad when it was delivered to his table. When he had finished it, the waiter brought him the steak. After a few bites, Igor pushed the plate aside and called the waiter.

"The steak is too rare!" he complained.

"Sir, would you like another steak—somewhere between medium and rare, perhaps?"

"No. I'm leaving now!"

Utterly confused, the waiter returned to the kitchen with Igor's plate.

"What the hell is going on?" Borovsky yelled when he saw the plate. "The son-of-a-bitch is a pain in the ass. Give the bastard the check so we can get rid of him."

The waiter hurriedly delivered Igor the check and waited for payment.

Igor looked up, stared at the server and said, "Not so fast. The steak was awful, but the salad was decent. My mother likes to cook and she is very fond of salads. Tell the chef I want the recipe for the dressing. It would be a nice gift for the old lady for her birthday."

Visibly perplexed, the waiter stepped into the kitchen and told Borovsky of the man's request.

"He wants the recipe for the salad dressing as a birthday present for his mother."

Borovsky angrily banged a large knife on the butcher-block and shouted, "Screw his mother! Tell that snotty fellow . . . *politely* . . . that I cannot give him the recipe."

The waiter returned to Igor's table once more. "Sorry, Sir. The chef is unable to give you the recipe for the dressing."

Removing his dark glasses and fixing his eyes sternly at the waiter, Igor said. "I see."

He got up, threw the money and a slip of paper with a phone number on the table and said, "Should the chef change his mind about the recipe, he will know how to reach me." Then he quickly left the restaurant without leaving a tip.

On his way back to OMNIA Igor worried about the failure of his mission and the tongue-lashing he was bound to get from his boss. He opened the liquor cabinet in the limousine and poured himself a vodka.

As soon as he was back, he went straight to Lamansky's suite and asked the secretary, "Can I see, Mr. Lamansky?"

"He is occupied right now," replied the secretary. "The red light on his door is on. When it turns green he is free."

Inside the office, Lamansky was on the phone. "Leonid, come on! Let's keep it simple. Ask the moron to drop the dough in a sealed envelope in the trash can in Gorki Park—you know, the one nearest the maintenance building. If he doesn't, you know what the next step is."

Outside the door, the green light came on. The secretary opened the door ajar to the boss' office and said, "Igor is here."

"Let him in."

Igor stepped into the office.

"Well, did you get the recipe?"

"No Sir, I'm sorry. Mr. Borovsky refused."

Frowning, Lamansky raised his voice. "I sent you on a simple mission and you failed. Your performance is totally unacceptable. If you want to advance in this organization you'll have to learn to do things right!"

With an air of distress, Igor replied, "Yes Sir."

After a tense moment of silence, Lamansky added. "I guess you know what the next step is. Look it up in our operations manual, *section 6, paragraph 11*, under the heading *Persuasion*. I certainly hope that you have studied this section which, as you know, is part of your curriculum."

"Yes Sir. I have."

Red-faced, Igor hurried through the corridors to his desk in the room where all the trainees were located. One of them noticed that Igor seemed downhearted.

"I guess you've been with the boss. Did he chew your ass?"

Igor didn't answer. He sat down at his desk, opened his operations manual and immersed himself in *section 6, paragraph 11*.

Chapter 7

When Borovsky arrived at his restaurant a few days after Igor's visit, to his horror, the large front window had been smashed. There was a brick on the floor and splintered glass all over the place. Stunned, he rushed to the telephone, grabbed the phonebook and feverishly turned the pages to find a company to install a new window. He found one and dialed their number.

"My window has to be replaced," he said. "Make it snappy. I've got customers coming in around noon!"

Still fuming with anger, Borovsky turned toward his old cleaning woman who was sweeping the glass splinters from the floor and roared. "This damned city is full of punks!" Then he left for the kitchen slamming the door shut.

About half an hour later, a van from OMNIA GLASS arrived and a new window was installed.

- - - -

When Borovsky arrived the next morning, he saw a small envelope on the floor. It had been pushed under the front door. He opened the envelope. Inside was a note saying:

Have you thought about it?

He sat down and read the note over and over.

"What the hell does it mean?" he asked himself. *Anyway*, he thought, *I have to report this to the police.*

He immediately left for the central police station and asked to see the police chief. After being searched by a police officer, he was led to the chief's office. He knocked on the door. A booming voice from inside told him to enter.

The chief was a hefty man sitting behind a large cluttered desk puffing on a cigar. The walls of the office were covered by soccer memorabilia. Framed photos showing individual players and team

29

POETRY AND UNDERWEAR AND OTHER STORIES

pictures filled every inch of the wall. A soccer ball with signatures on it sat on his desk.

"My name is Jaroslav Borovsky."

"I'm Chief Stransky."

"Chief, I see that you are a big soccer fan."

"Yes, and I'm a keen supporter of Dynamo. It's my favorite team. I go to all their matches, even away games. The last match I saw was against Kiev. It was a very exciting game. Kiev was leading by two goals with five minutes to play. But then, thank God, Dynamo was awarded a penalty kick and Marat, the mid-fielder, put it right in the lower left corner of the goal. No chance for the keeper. With less than a minute left, Carlos, our Brazilian star, headed the ball in the goal off a corner kick. It was beautiful. So, it was a tie. Dynamo should have won. They controlled most of the play but unfortunately, missed several scoring chances. Mr. Borovsky, are you also interested in soccer?"

Although Borovsky had no interest whatsoever, he thought, *I better sound positive.*

"Yes, Chief, but my restaurant ties me down. We are open each day of the week. I have to be there to cook and supervise my personnel. I've watched a few matches on television and I agree with you, Dynamo is a great team!"

Borovsky, tired of all the soccer talk and anxious to get to the matter at hand, continued. "Chief, it's about my restaurant."

"Yes, I know your place. I've eaten there a few times with my family. I'm very fond of one of your salad dishes. I think it's called something like Kremlin Salad. What can I do for you?"

"Yesterday morning when I arrived at my restaurant, the large window was smashed and this morning I found this note." He handed it to the chief who read it.

"I see a connection between the damage to your window and the note. Tell me, Mr. Borovsky, can you think of anybody having a grudge against you?"

"Well maybe. A young arrogant fellow had lunch in my restaurant a few days ago. He raised hell about the steak he ordered—didn't like the way it was cooked, and it was my best meat—real tender. He also had a salad and wanted the recipe for the dressing. I refused to give it to him."

The police chief smothered his cigar butt in the ashtray, lit a new one and leaned back in his chair.

"What did that man look like?"

"He was elegantly dressed in a black suit. He wore dark glasses and arrived in a stretch limousine with chauffeur."

"Aha," said the chief, "it was probably a member of a gangster organization. We have quite a few of those goons here in Moscow. It's difficult to get a handle on them and their activities. They hide behind legitimate businesses. But, for the life of me, I cannot see why some punk who didn't like your meat and could not get your recipe, would smash your window and threaten you. These criminals would not go to such lengths. They are involved in much bigger things."

The chief, puffing vigorously on his cigar continued, "Is there anyone else who in the past has been interested in getting your recipe?"

"Oh yes. Several months ago an American—a Jerry Sweikert, who had lunch in my place, asked for it. I refused. I remember that he owns a restaurant."

"I see," said the chief. "I think I've got it. It may well be that the American fellow is behind this thing. He has probably hired that hoodlum to get the recipe for him."

"Do you really think so?"

"Yes, and I'm not surprised. These Americans have deep pockets and they would not shy away from paying some gangster to get what they want. If I were you, I would give that goon the recipe to avoid any more headaches."

"No way, Chief! That will be over my dead body!"

"It may well be so," the chief said thoughtfully. "But if you insist on pursuing this matter, and it's likely that a foreign national is involved, I regret we cannot be of any help. It is, in my opinion, an international case which is the domain of the KGB, our secret police."

The chief got up from his chair and led Borovsky toward the door.

"By the way," he said. "Dynamo is playing at home here in Moscow next Saturday against Sevastopol. You ought to see that match. It's going to be a great one!"

Dismayed, Borovsky left the police station. On his way back to the restaurant, he thought, *this is absurd. I go to the police about a crime and all I hear from that dope of a police chief is his babbling about soccer.*

Chapter 8

The next day Borovsky found an envelope inside the front door of his restaurant. In it was a note. It read:

Drop the recipe for the salad dressing at exactly 11 o'clock tonight in the trash container nearest the toilets in Sadusky Park. Must be in a sealed envelope inside the enclosed plastic bag. Do not alert anyone or else you and your family will be harmed.

Borovsky studied the note. "These bastards are not getting my recipe," he said to himself. "I'm going to fool them. They are getting a fake one. That will screw up things for the American *and* the goon, and they will give up pestering me."

He wrote down a recipe, put in an envelope, sealed it, and slid it into the plastic bag. Around 10:30 that evening, he took a bus to Sadusky Park. He was not very familiar with the park. It had been years since he had been there. Walking around in the darkness trying to locate the toilets, he saw a hobo sound asleep on a bench. He shook the poor fellow to wake him up.

Grumbling and groggy, the vagrant turned around and said, "Can't you see, I'm sleeping? What do you want?"

"I'm sorry to wake you, but could you tell me where the toilets are?"

Half asleep, the man mumbled, "You see where the paths cross over there? Take a left, go about fifty meters until you come to another crossing. Take a left again and you will see a statue. I think it's old Lenin's. Then turn right and you will see the toilets ahead. There's never any toilet paper. I hope you brought your own!

Then the man turned his back to Borovsky. "Don't disturb me anymore, I need my sleep!"

Borovsky found the toilets and the trash receptacle. He dropped the plastic bag in it. All of a sudden, he felt a pressing need to use the facilities. He entered the toilet, sat down, and discovered to his dismay that the homeless fellow was right—there was no toilet paper.

- - - -

Anxiously awaiting news from OMNIA about the recipe Jerry remained sequestered in his room. He alternated between lying on the bed and pacing around, with frequent trips to the bathroom. An empty vodka bottle sat on the bedside table. Finally, the phone rang.

"Mr. Sweikert, Mr. Lamansky wants to see you," said the telephone operator. "He asks that you to come to our offices tomorrow at 10 o'clock. I suggest you take a cab."

"I'll be there," Jerry replied.

- - - -

The next morning Jerry arrived at OMNIA's offices. After the usual frisking, he reached the front office of Lamansky's suite and sat down in the waiting room. The secretary looked up at the door to the boss' office and said, "When the green light is on, he is free."

After a few minutes, the light changed.

"Mr. Sweikert, Mr. Lamansky is free. You can enter now."

When Jerry stepped into the office, Lamansky was all smiles.

"Here is the recipe," he said, handing Jerry an envelope. "We have translated the recipe into English. I guess this settles the matter. Satisfaction is always guaranteed whenever anyone comes to us for assistance. And, young Igor did a good job. I always knew this fellow had talent."

Lamansky called his secretary and said, "Ask personnel to send Igor over to my office, now!"

Moments later Igor arrived and entered Lamansky's office.

"Igor, you did a fine job in getting the recipe for Mr. Sweikert. You are due for a raise next month. Keep up the good work!"

"Thank you, Sir," Igor responded and left the office.

Turning toward Jerry, Lamansky said, "That wasn't *that* difficult."

They shook hands and Jerry left OMNIA's offices with the recipe in his pocket.

He went straight to the reception desk at the hotel. He showed the recipe to the clerk and said, "I got the recipe, but there is no English word for one of the ingredients. What is it?"

The clerk read the recipe. "I know what it is. It's a spice called tugor. It's often used here in Russia for baking. You can get it and all the other ingredients in any supermarket."

"Could I borrow a couple of bowls, a hand mixer and a few spoons from the kitchen?" Jerry asked.

"Certainly. We'll have it brought to your room right away."

A few blocks away Jerry found a supermarket. All the items needed were available there. He returned to the hotel and on entering his room, he saw the kitchenware on a table. He sat down and read the recipe very carefully. It was very detailed and showed the various ratios. The recipe also indicated that after mixing, the dressing should be refrigerated for at least two hours before use.

After preparing the mixture, he placed it in the small refrigerator in the room and lay down on the bed to relax. To be on the safe side, should he doze off, he set the alarm clock to ring when the salad dressing was ready.

Too tense to fall asleep, Jerry jumped from the bed when the clock finally rang. Carefully he removed the dressing from the refrigerator, placed it on the table, and sat down to taste it. He scooped up a tablespoon of the mixture and moved it around in his mouth while looking up at the ceiling in deep concentration.

Grimacing he yelled, "I'll be damned! I've been had!"

With a feeling of helplessness, he sat down on the bed and buried his head in his hands. "What do I do now?" he asked himself. "I've spent over a thousand dollars on this thing, wasted a lot of time, and here I sit with that disgusting dressing." He got up, went to the bathroom, threw the mixture in the toilet, and flushed.

Jerry spent the rest of the day in his room thinking about what to do next. He was getting fed up with the run-around, and seriously thought of dropping the idea of ever getting the recipe. OMNIA had not lived up to their motto of guaranteed satisfaction. He felt that at least, they had to be told.

- - - -

The next morning he phoned OMNIA to arrange another appointment with Lamansky.

"Just a moment, Mr. Sweikert," the secretary said. "I'll check with him."

She opened the door to Lamansky's office and said. "Mr. Sweikert is on the phone. He would like to see you again."

"What! I thought that stupid salad dressing affair had been settled. Quite frankly, I've had it with this thing. Tell that American I've no time to meet with him now and I don't know when it may be possible. That will stop him from pestering me about this silly matter. Tell him that since Igor has been involved in this project, we'll send him to the hotel as our representative."

The secretary picked up the phone and relayed the message to Jerry.

"When can he come?" Jerry asked.

"Right away," she replied.

- - - -

Igor arrived at the hotel, this time by taxi. Under his arm, he carried the operations manual. He met Jerry in the lobby.

"Mr. Sweikert, Mr. Lamansky sent me to talk with you. Are there any problems?"

Exasperated Jerry answered, "Yes, there are! The recipe for the salad dressing was a fake. I mixed the salad dressing myself and tasted it. It was awful, a far cry from Borovsky's recipe. Is there anything further that can be done? Do you have any suggestions?" Jerry asked.

Igor opened the operations manual, flipped the pages as if he was searching for a solution.

"Mr. Sweikert, in this manual there are many alternatives," Igor said. "Let me give you some examples. Most small businesses in Russia, like restaurants, cheat on both income and sales taxes. We could put Borovsky on notice that unless he gives us the correct recipe, we will arrange for tax audits of his books. Most merchants hate that."

Igor continued reading the manual. "*Or*, we could try another brick, if you know what I mean. We could kidnap him or a member of his family and hold them hostage until the recipe is secured. This is a complicated operation. The question is whether it would work in this case. The fee is pretty high too. Anyway, let me discuss a possible next step with Mr. Lamansky. He makes all major decisions."

35

"Thanks, Igor, for stopping by. In the meantime, I will give this matter some thought myself."

Igor left the hotel and Jerry went back to his room. Sitting on the bed, he reflected on Igor's visit. The alternatives suggested by the Russian struck him as being far too dramatic. He was also running out of money. If he stayed much longer in Moscow, he would probably not even have enough cash to pay his hotel bill. He had already been informed that the hotel didn't accept credit cards.

Chapter 9

Igor had returned to OMNIA. He went straight to Lamansky's office.

"Sir, Mr. Sweikert told me the recipe that was dropped off in the park was a fake. He mixed the recipe and tasted the dressing."

Frowning, Lamansky became serious, "This Borovsky fellow is playing games with us. I don't like that. Although I've had enough of this stupid matter, no one is going to screw around with this organization and go unpunished. Our reputation is at stake."

"Mr. Lamansky, what do you think we should do?"

"We don't want to waste any more resources on this idiotic thing. However, we need to send Borovsky another brick as a farewell gift." Then he added with a smile, "Our window replacement division will make another sale. Igor, take care of this."

"Yes, Sir."

During the night, another brick was hurled through the window of Borovsky's restaurant.

"Blasted thugs!" Borovsky bellowed when he discovered the mess in the morning.

Again, he phoned to have the window replaced. He waited for days for another note, but no new message followed the brick. With a feeling of relief, he muttered to himself, "I beat these bastards. They have given up."

Meanwhile, Jerry, disheartened that his quest for Borovsky's salad dressing recipe had been in vain, decided to leave Moscow for home. He booked a ticket for the first available flight back to the United States. When the plane was airborne, he looked down as the skyline of Moscow faded out of sight. He leaned back in his seat, and with a sigh said to himself, "I hope I never see that damned city again."

Chapter 10

Each year, *Pravda*, the largest and most influential newspaper in Russia, selects Restaurant of the Year. The news of the award is broadcast all over Russia in the press and on television. To Borovsky's surprise, his restaurant was awarded this prestigious honor because of the quality, variety of food, and the value it offers its guests.

Soon after the announcement, the press flocked to the restaurant. TV trucks were parked outside in the street, which was cordoned off to accommodate reporters and cameramen with their equipment. Inside the restaurant, cameras and large lamps were set up, and long lines of cables were strung across the floor. There was so much traffic that Borovsky had to close the restaurant for the day. Print and TV journalists were falling over each other, eager to get interviews with him.

A reporter from a major television station muscled his way through the crowd.

"Congratulations! Mr. Borovsky. All eyes of Russia are on you on this special occasion. What do you think was the reason your establishment was selected?"

"Well, I think my menu is good and diverse. If I were to single out one dish, it has to be my *Salad a la Kremlin*. It's a big hit."

Seizing the opportunity to stick it to the police chief for his inability to help him, he added, "My salad dish has caused me a lot of headaches."

"How come?" asked the reporter.

"Someone has been harassing and threatening me and my family to get the recipe for the dressing. Because I refused, the front window in my restaurant has been smashed twice by bricks. I went to the police and reported the first incident to Chief Stransky, but was met by impotence on his part to investigate the matter. He suspected a foreign national might have hired the Mafia to get the recipe. He referred me to the KGB. The chief even suggested that I should consider giving in and hand over the recipe to these hoodlums to avoid any more problems."

"Who could that foreigner be?"

"Several months ago an American by the name of Sweikert, who owns a restaurant in America, was very interested in getting the recipe. I refused. Shortly after, a young thug–no doubt a member of the Mafia—made a scene in my restaurant and demanded the recipe. Again, I refused. Then a brick was hurled through the window and a second one, recently, ruined it again."

- - - -

The following day, the interview with Borovsky was featured all over Russia. It was big news. Screaming headlines read, *American Industrial Espionage*, *American Hires Mafia*, and *The Salad Dressing Affair*. Newspapers were outdoing each other as they dramatized the story. The Mafia boss, unaware that Jerry had already left Russia, saw the interview with Borovsky on the TV news program and called a meeting with his top lieutenants.

"You fellows have probably seen the interview with that clown Borovsky. I'm thoroughly disgusted with this salad dressing matter. The whole thing is a joke. It's potentially a hot potato for us. I forbid anyone in our organization to have anything to do with that idiot, Sweikert. This whole mess could expose us and blow up in our faces. Instruct our security people to deny that dope any access to our premises and tell our telephone operators to hang up should he call us. I hope I've made myself clear! You can leave now."

Chief Savansky had seen the Borovsky interview too. Sitting in his living room, he mumbled to himself, "This moron accuses me of impotence. I have fathered three boys and two girls." He turned toward his wife. "Dear, don't you think we have a good sex life?"

Without looking up from her knitting work, she replied, "It's all right."

- - - -

The corridors of the huge KGB headquarters were buzzing with activity. Everybody was talking about the salad dressing espionage incident. Jokes were cracked and loud laughter was audible throughout the massive complex.

Nicolas Benin, the KGB Director, summoned his number two to his office.

"Ivan, you are probably aware of all the commotion caused by this laughable salad dressing story. People are going nuts about it. You know, Ivan, for a long time, this place has been awfully quiet—indeed, much *too* quiet. Our organization has been hibernating for far too long. This thing could be juicy. Our usual job of keeping the opposition to our government in check is pretty much a cakewalk. We need to spread our wings. This affair is a golden opportunity for us to shine while sticking it to the Americans. For too long, our relations with our friends at the CIA have been rather placid. It's time we rock the boat and embarrass them. I will contact their head man to get the ball rolling with this."

Chapter 11

Across the Atlantic, at the CIA Headquarters near Washington, D.C., John Smith, the Director, was munching on a hamburger. He had told his secretary never to disturb him during his lunch break. Suddenly his door opened and his secretary stuck her head in.

"Mr. Smith, the Russians are on the phone!"

"Tell those communists to phone back later. I'm having lunch!"

"But Sir, Mr. Benin, the Director of the KGB, is on the line."

"Damn. Put him on!"

"Hi Nick, what's up? I haven't heard from you for a long time. What's happening on the Eastern Front?"

"Well, John, we have an espionage case here involving an American. His name is Sweikert. He owns a restaurant in Cincinnati."

"Tell me about it!"

"This Sweikert fellow apparently hired the mob here to get a salad dressing recipe from a local restaurant. The owner refused to surrender it and then the window of his restaurant was smashed twice. Also, he and his family were threatened by the Mafia. Since it's one of *your* dear countrymen, I thought you would like to know what happened."

"You must be kidding, Nick! It's absurd that our two organizations should get involved in a silly matter about a salad dressing recipe!"

"True John, but this thing is all over Russia—in the press, on TV, *and* my government knows about it. We have to get this matter under control for the sake of the relatively good relations between our two countries. What do you suggest we do?"

"Expel the son-of-a-bitch! Let's make sure this moronic thing is not blown out of proportion!"

"Okay, John. I'll have my agents pick him up at his hotel and put him on the first flight home."

- - - -

The next day, two KGB agents turned up at the hotel with handcuffs at the ready. Approaching the desk clerk, one of the agents said, "We are here to pick up a man by the name of Jerry Sweikert."

"*Oh*, the American. He left several days ago. He was an odd fellow. He made salad dressing in his room."

Perplexed, the agent looked at his colleague. "It's weird. We were sent here to seize a man because he made *salad dressing* in his room?"

- - - -

The salad dressing affair had hit the headlines in the United States as well. Cartoonists had a field day with it. Talk show hosts and stand-up comedians were dishing up jokes and parodies. The State Department's damage control apparatus went into overdrive to diffuse the situation. Even the White House and Congress were notified and kept abreast through daily briefings.

The President was sitting in the Oval Office watching football on television when his chief of staff opened the door and said, "Mr. President, I have a briefing paper for you regarding the salad dressing controversy."

"I'm too busy to read it, and I don't want to hear anything more about that dumb thing. After years of strained relations with these commies, the arms race, the missile crisis and political skirmishes with them, we have finally entered a period of détente. Now all hell is breaking loose because of a salad dressing. Tell all the department secretaries and the CIA to stay away from that crap. I don't want anyone to spend any more time on it. And, don't disturb me again! The Steelers are leading the Rams by three points with only twelve seconds left in the game!"

Chapter 12

Years passed and ripples from the old salad dressing affair had long ago died down. U.S.-Russia relations were never adversely affected.

Jerry accepted the fact that all the twists and turns in his attempts to get Borovsky's legendary salad dressing recipe had been in vain and that he would never get his hands on it. With this matter behind him, he concentrated all his efforts on his business. He expanded his restaurant and opened additional outlets in Cincinnati and all over Ohio. His enterprise grew at a rapid clip and became very profitable.

It reached a point when it was increasingly difficult for him to expand and manage his empire, so he decided to franchise. Many entrepreneurs signed up. In the process, Jerry became a man of substantial wealth. He moved into a large mansion in the outskirts of Cincinnati and bought a condominium in Florida. Recognition as Businessman of the Year followed, and he became a major donor to a host of charities.

The U.S. President, a Republican, was nearing the end of his first term in office and it was time for him to run for re-election to a second term.

Jerry Sweikert became a major donor to the Republican presidential re-election effort, and an active and successful fundraiser as well. His wealth, influence and empire of restaurants gave him enormous visibility. The Democratic candidate's handlers attempted to make a big deal out of Jerry's involvement in the old espionage affair . . . without much success.

The Republican candidate won the re-election by a landslide—in no small measure due to the contributions and efforts by big donors like Jerry Sweikert. After the election, he was invited to several inauguration festivities, rubbing shoulders with dignitaries and other major players in the campaign. He shook hands with the president and a photo session with him received extensive press coverage.

Customarily, during the second term of an administration, many top government jobs are awarded to major donors or cronies of the president. Among these new appointments were several cushy ambassadorships, which are often given to individuals, who, in one way or another, have played significant roles in the campaign. When it was time for the president to review the list of potential candidates to head the diplomatic missions abroad, Jerry's name was included.

As the President sat in the Oval Office, reviewing ambassadorial appointments with his chief of staff, Jerry's name came up.

"Mr. President, I would strongly recommend that we give Mr. Sweikert an ambassadorial post," the aide said.

"No way," replied the President. "Don't you remember? This was the guy who nearly ruined our relationship with the Russians over that stupid salad dressing affair."

"True, Mr. President. Nevertheless, you won the crucial swing state of Ohio handily because of his hard work. You have to do *something* to reward him. After all, he raised nearly $30 million for you!"

"OK. Give him a small post in Europe—like Mali."

"Excuse me Sir, but Mali is an African country. I suggest we give him the Moscow job. After all, he has been there a couple of times. He got to know the environment there and the Russian people. One thing he has going for him is his restaurant background. We don't have to send him to etiquette school to learn how to eat properly with fork and knife. As you know, Sir, many of our envoys have in the past had some table manner problems."

With an air of skepticism, the President countered. "I question whether this is a good idea. How would the Russian government react? I'm sure the old controversy is still on their minds."

"Mr. President, that was years ago. It's old news. The Russians have no doubt already forgotten the matter. In my opinion, we should not pay attention to what they think. We should not let them dictate what we should or should *not* do."

"All right, give him Moscow. But tell State Department to keep a close eye on him."

- - - -

A few days later Jerry got a call from the President's chief of staff summoning him to Washington for an interview. He flew immediately to Dulles Airport and arrived at the White House by taxi. A presidential aide steered him to the office of the chief of staff.

"Welcome to the White House, Mr. Sweikert. The President is very appreciative of your efforts on his behalf during the recent presidential elections. He wants to chat with you. Let's go over to the Oval Office."

On reaching the sanctuary, the chief of staff tapped lightly on the door and opened it.

"Mr. President, Mr. Sweikert is here to see you."

The television was on in the Oval Office and the President, sitting in front of it, turned around and said, "Wait outside a few minutes. The Falcons are at fourth down and have opted for a field goal. Stupid! Why don't they go for it?"

The chief of staff gently closed the door and waited outside for the signal to enter.

"You can come in now!" roared the President.

"Have a seat, gentlemen," said the President while glancing at the television set. Then he turned around facing the two men.

"Mr. Sweikert, thank you for your help in my re-election campaign."

"Don't mention it Mr. President. I always knew that you were the right man to continue to lead our nation through the difficult times ahead."

A moment of silence followed and Jerry nervously changed his position in his chair.

"Mr. Sweikert," intoned the President, "My chief of staff has recommended that you be appointed ambassador to Moscow. Although I have an open mind, I must be frank with you, I'm mindful of your involvement in an old controversy there. I'm sure you know what I'm talking about."

"Yes, Mr. President, but allow me to say that the controversial episode happened years ago. I was young and it was a case of youthful indiscretion on my part. I learned a lesson Sir, and if given the post, I shall dedicate myself day and night to vigorously defend and protect the interest of our country."

"Well said, Mr. Sweikert," muttered the President. "Well then, congratulations! But promise me that you will never eat in that restaurant again. We don't want any more problems with those Russians."

"Mr. President, I assure you that I never will."

They got up and shook hands. The president turned his attention back toward the TV, and Jerry and the chief of staff left the Oval Office.

Chapter 13

The position as ambassador to Russia is one of the most important diplomatic posts in the Foreign Service. The news of Jerry's appointment caused quite a stir. Dailies and TV reported on it and a flurry of editorials appeared.

The old salad dressing affair was still fresh in the memory of the media. Many questioned the wisdom of assigning a person with such a questionable background to this important post. Some jokingly asked what the cook from Cincinnati was up to next.

Headlines like *Lover of Salad Dressing posted to Russia*, *Goose Cooked in Moscow* and *Diplomacy Cooked* appeared in the press. Talk show hosts cracked one-liners about Jerry Sweikert's appointment and cartoonists seized upon the subject, adding amusement to the choice of Jerry as a top diplomat.

Diplomatic appointments are the prerogative of the administration, and do not require confirmation by Congress. However, Jerry's nomination created tumultuous scenes there. Democrats, who controlled both houses, loudly condemned the choice as an example of the Republican administration running amok.

- - - -

In Russia, Jerry's appointment to Moscow was big news as well. Like in the U.S., it caused a lively debate in the media. But, whereas the treatment in the American media of the choice of Jerry Sweikert for the job was a blend of criticism, sarcasm and light-hearted observations, Russian reaction was skeptical, even outright hostile.

The KGB briefed the Russian President in detail about the old espionage incident and warned him of potential troubles ahead. He resigned himself to the fact that it was a *fait accompli*. However, he instructed the KGB to keep a watchful eye on the activities of the new American ambassador.

- - - -

47

On Jerry's arrival at Moscow Airport, a black limousine with a uniformed chauffeur and an American flag on the hood transported him to the ambassadorial residence. When the vehicle reached the iron gated entrance, two U.S. Marines saluted, and the automatic gate opened. The residence was a stately mansion. Jerry was awestruck by its ornate beauty. He was later told that it was once the home of a high-ranking general and close associate of a former Tsar. Unfortunately, the poor officer was executed during the Russian Revolution. The residence was staffed with a valet, driver, two maids, a male cook, and a gardener.

When not at the embassy, Jerry spent a lot of time in the kitchen with the cook. He had been in the service of a number of former ambassadors over the years. He was reluctant to adopt Jerry's suggestions to include more American food in the daily menus.

"Mr. Ambassador," he said, "I have been trained in preparing international food—mainly French and Italian cuisines, and all the guests like it. I don't know anything about American dishes."

"Never mind what you have done in the past. I'll show you," said Jerry. He handed the cook a folder of his recipes and said, "Please study these recipes, and if you have any questions I'll help you out."

While at home, the apron-clad ambassador spent many hours in the kitchen manipulating pots and pans—introducing the cook to American cuisine. Hamburgers, hot-dogs, barbecue, yams, hush-puppies, cornbread, and bread pudding, along with a great number of casserole dishes, paraded in front of the skeptical and condescending eyes of the old cook.

One day on inspecting the grounds surrounding the residence, Jerry came upon a shed in the corner of the large lawn. He noticed a strange smell. "What is this for?" he asked the valet.

"The former ambassador was a sheep farmer—I think from North Dakota. He built the shed and raised lambs. We ate a lot of the meat here. Many Muslims came here, mainly around their holy festivities like Ramadan, to buy the lambs."

It's funny, Jerry mused, *the Foreign Services recruits are some real odd balls.*

Chapter 14

When it was time for Jerry to present his credentials to the Russian President, his limousine brought him to the Kremlin complex. He was met by a high-ranking government official who escorted him through long corridors and several doors, to the office suite of the Russian head of state. He entered the suite and was greeted by the President.

"Mr. Ambassador, welcome to Moscow! I hope you have settled down well in our fair city."

"Yes, thank you, Mr. President."

"I understand you have visited Moscow before," and with a tinge of humor he added, "*And* that you like the food here."

"Yes, Mr. President, I have fond memories of my earlier visits here years ago."

Anxious to return to protocol, Jerry intoned in a lofty voice, "I'm pleased to convey to you, Mr. President, and to the Russian people, the warmest personal greetings from the President of United States and the American people, *and* the wishes of my government that the friendly relations between our two nations will always remain strong and constructive."

Jerry handed the President a large envelope containing his official credentials. The President opened it and without looking at the content, he handed it to an aide.

"Well, Mr. Ambassador, let's retire to my study to chat," the President said.

The two gentlemen settled into deep leather chairs in the exquisitely appointed library.

"Mr. Ambassador, after numerous tumultuous periods in our relationship, our countries have entered into an era of mutual understanding and cordiality. It's my fervent hope that working together, hand in hand, this shared good will can be strengthened further. I'm convinced that your presence here in Russia will further enhance the collaboration between our two countries for the betterment of the world. I hope you share this view, Mr. Ambassador."

"Certainly, Mr. President," Jerry answered.

"Mr. Ambassador let's have a drink. What would you like?"

"I would love a vodka, thanks."

"I'll have one too," said the President.

Then he rang a bell and soon after, a valet appeared with the drinks.

"Mr. President, how are things going in Russia?" Jerry asked.

The President became serious as he downed his drink. "Like any other country, we have, of course, internal problems. The opposition to my government is very active and loud. There is a perception among a large part of our population that our administration is inefficient and corrupt. It's true that we have had to imprison some high-level bureaucrats in charge of some of our major state-owned industries. We also had to close a few newspapers that had been spreading exaggerated, even false, rumors about widespread graft within my government. What has added to our headaches is the mad rush to a free-market economy."

The president took another drink of his vodka and continued. "I think my predecessors were too quick in changing our past entrenched state-run economy into an untested free-market system. We probably should have eased into economic reforms gradually over time. This has created all sorts of problems. Many unscrupulous entrepreneurs took advantage of the situation, milking unsuspecting investors, big and small, through fraudulent schemes, promising high returns from companies that did not even exist.

"As a result, we probably have the highest number of multi-millionaires *and* poor people in Europe. We are trying to get our run-amok economy under control, but our attempts at reform are met with stiff resistance from a powerful segment of the business community and 'old guard' bureaucrats. Also, all this economic freedom has caused crime to rise, and gangs, like the Mafia—which we never had before—are strangling a substantial part of our economy."

"Mr. President, what about democratic reforms?"

"Although we want to introduce more democratic reforms, we have to go slow because a rush to full democracy may, in fact, make our current problems worse."

"Mr. President, don't feel bad about this. Some of the Founding Fathers of my country were hostile toward democracy and warned against its excesses. In fact, one of them, John Adams, our second President, said that democracy never lasts long and eventually commits suicide. I can well appreciate, Mr. President, that you have a lot on your plate, but be assured that my government stands squarely behind you in your efforts to reform Russian society."

"Thank you, Mr. Ambassador, I appreciate that."

They had another vodka, exchanged handshakes, and Jerry left the office. As soon as he had returned to the embassy, Jerry told his secretary to transmit a coded message to the State Department containing the information just obtained from the Russian President.

Jerry's relationship with the Russian President grew and they became very close friends. Both of them had a weakness for vodka. They often met informally at night, in the presidential suite, in the Kremlin, and the vodka was flowing.

"Let's drop the titles. Call me Stanislav," the President said in a slurred voice, after an evening of heavy drinking.

"I'll call you Stan," Jerry said to the President as he staggered over to the bar for another drink. "Is that okay with you?"

"Yes Jerry. Let's drink to that!"

- - - -

At the embassy, Jerry became very popular because of his folksy and jovial manners. After working for years under rather staid ambassadors, the staff was elated to have an informal and jocular Head of Mission. Jerry would often bring hamburgers, barbecue, and cornbread to the embassy for lunch and shared these delicacies with his personnel.

All ambassadors were instructed by their governments what to say and what *not* to say, when in the company of Russian officials and fellow ambassadors from other countries. They followed the directives from home to the letter. Whenever one nation had strained relations with another, its ambassador was, at times, instructed to avoid the other country's envoy at diplomatic receptions and cocktail parties.

Whenever Jerry received similar instructions, he happily ignored them as he moved around in freewheeling fashion on the diplomatic circuit. In the beginning, the diplomatic corps looked upon Jerry with a jaundiced eye, but little by little, they warmed up to his informality and his popularity grew. Through his informal chats, off the cuff, with other ambassadors and Russian officials, he gathered a lot of information—most of it irrelevant. He relayed all of it to Washington in a steady stream of messages.

The State Department had to increase its personnel to cope with the huge amount of information from Moscow, and sift out what was of interest and what was totally irrelevant. Chatty remarks about food preferences of the various ambassadors drove the State Department up the wall. The fact that the Greek envoy did not like Greek Salad, and his German counterpart hated sauerkraut, was of no interest to Washington. It reached a point when Jerry was admonished by the State Department only to submit relevant information of a political nature.

Chapter 15

One day while sitting in his office, Jerry got a phone call from the Russian President.

"Jerry, how are you doing?"

"Fine, Stan, what about you?"

"Well, we have a bothersome family problem which I would like to discuss with you. What would you think about spending next weekend with me and my wife in our dacha in the country away from Moscow? Can you make it?"

"Certainly, I would be delighted!"

"All right then, I will send a limousine to pick you up Saturday morning at eight o'clock."

- - - -

At the appointed time, a limousine arrived equipped with Russian and American flags on the hood. Settling into the car, Jerry poured himself a vodka from the bar inside.

Why would he invite me? He wondered. *Maybe it's something big—perhaps an important matter affecting U.S./Russian relations.*

On his arrival at the villa, Jerry was greeted by Stanislav and his wife.

"Welcome Jerry. Please, meet my wife Renata."

"Glad to know you, ma'am," Jerry obliged.

They entered a large living room and sat down.

"So, Stan, what's on your mind?"

"Jerry, let me explain. Our family is facing a serious problem. Our daughter, Elena, got married about a year ago, and we fear her marriage is already on the rocks."

"Why?" Jerry asked.

"She is a terrible cook, and we suspect, even fear, that her husband, Mikail, will leave her. He is a gourmand, and almost every evening he's away from their apartment eating with friends in restaurants all over Moscow. And, Elena sits alone in their home waiting for him to return, which is always very late. It's a terrible dilemma for Elena. I understand that you, Jerry, have a restaurant background and know how to cook. We are absolutely convinced that if Elena could cook good dishes for her husband, their marriage could be saved. Would it be possible for you to give her cooking lessons?"

"Sure, I could do that, but I'm not familiar with Russian food."

"Never mind, American or international cuisine would do." He smiled and added, "Russian food is for the birds, anyway. It's not very exciting. If it's okay with you, I will ask Elena to come here tomorrow, so we can discuss the matter."

"That'll be fine, Stan," Jerry responded.

- - - -

Elena arrived at the dacha the following morning. Stanislav greeted her in the doorway and led her into the living room.

"Elena, please meet Mr. Sweikert, the American ambassador."

"Glad to meet you, Sir," she said.

"Elena, the ambassador is a chef in his civilian life and he has a thorough knowledge of cooking. I think he could be of help."

Somewhat disoriented, Elena thought to herself, *this fellow is a diplomat and he can cook. So what?*

A moment of tense silence ensued. Then Stanislav addressed his daughter. "Elena, please do not get upset about what I'm about to say. But, my impression is that you might need a little help with your cooking. The ambassador would be prepared to help you refine your culinary ability."

"You must be joking, Papa. The only food Americans know to cook is hamburgers and hotdogs!"

Taken back by this observation, Jerry felt he had to intervene.

"Miss Elena, over the years, the American palate has undergone an extensive refinement and today our standard of cooking is at least on par with French and Italian cuisines."

Then Stanislav, smiling, said, "Elena, unless you want to be exposed to Siberian cuisine, I would strongly urge you to accept the ambassador's offer. And I'm sure Mikail would welcome an improvement in your cooking."

"Papa, I know I'm not the greatest cook. I don't mind that Mikail sometimes eats out with friends. Quite frankly, I have no particular interest in cooking! I certainly hope he married me because he loves me—whether I can cook or *not.*"

"This may well be so, Elena, but when the honeymoon period is over, there are things that can, in the long run, add spice to any marriage and hold it together. One of these is good food."

With an air of reluctance, she sighed. "Okay, Papa."

Stanislav rose from his chair and said, "Well, that settles this matter. Let's have a drink. What would you like Jerry?"

"A vodka please."

"And you, Elena?"

"A Coke."

Arrangements were made for Jerry to give Elena lessons twice a week in the afternoon at her apartment.

At the beginning, Elena was not very receptive. But little by little, she warmed up to Jerry's instructions and her interest in cooking grew. Over time, she made good progress in preparing a variety of tasty dishes. On these cooking days, Jerry left the embassy early in the afternoon. He had told his secretary he was giving the Russian President's daughter cooking lessons.

Chapter 16

Back in Washington, the State Department was alerted to rumors of unrest in Chechnya, one of the Russian provinces. They needed to contact Jerry to find out what was going on. The Secretary of State phoned the Moscow mission. He got the embassy secretary on the line.

"This is the Secretary of State, please connect me with Mr. Sweikert, I have to talk to him!"

"I'm sorry, the ambassador is not available," the secretary replied.

"What do you mean, not available?"

"He is giving cooking lessons."

"Cooking lessons? To whom?" the Secretary of State asked in a demanding tone.

"The Russian President's daughter."

The Secretary of State, now very impatient, raised his voice, "I must speak with him right away. It's an urgent matter!"

"I'm sorry Sir, but I don't know how to contact him. I have no telephone number where he can be reached."

"This is ridiculous!" he yelled and hung up.

The Secretary of State immediately phoned the President in the Oval Office.

"Charlie, I cannot get in touch with our ambassador in Moscow about the Chechnya situation. He is away from the embassy giving the Russian President's daughter cooking lessons."

"What the hell is going on in your department? This fellow started off well and now the moron is absent from his post, *cooking!* I'll personally phone that idiot at his residence when it's night in Moscow to wake him up and take him to task!"

- - - -

Jerry was fast asleep when the telephone rang in the middle of the night. He woke up, stumbled out of bed and reached for the receiver. Groggy from sleep he muttered a weak "Hello?"

"Mr. Sweikert, this is the President speaking. Yesterday, the Secretary of State tried to reach you about an important political matter—a rumored unrest in Chechnya. He was told that you were absent from the embassy giving cooking lessons. Don't you understand that the post in Moscow is one of the most important within our foreign service? You have shown gross dereliction of duty. It's totally unacceptable!"

"But, Mr. President, the Russian President pleaded with me to give his daughter, Elena, cooking lessons. She couldn't cook, and because of that, her marriage was coming apart. She is now making very good progress in her cooking and, as I understand it, harmony between her and her husband Mikail is being restored. And we have only one session left."

The President, now very irate, tore into Jerry. "I don't give a rat's ass whether her marriage is going to pot. It's not our job to run around wiping the butts of those commies. That's not part of your job description. Do you understand?"

"Yes, Mr. President, but the Russian President has become a close friend, and I felt I had to help him solve a family problem. Also, I thought by doing so, the relations between our country and Russia would benefit."

"Bullshit," retorted the President. "They have to solve their *own* problems. It's not up to us to nanny them! As it's apparent that you cannot get into your little skull why you were posted to Moscow, I will immediately instruct the Secretary of State to find a replacement for you. You will hear direct from State about this!"

Jerry sat down on the bed reflecting on the tongue-lashing by the President. Then he crept into bed but could not fall asleep. He got up, poured himself a vodka, drank it and dozed off.

Chapter 17

Little by little, Mikail noticed a major improvement in Elena's cooking ability and was gladly surprised by the variety of tasty dishes she served him for dinner.

"How come you cook so well now, Elena?" he asked.

"The American ambassador has been giving me lessons."

"Wow, a high-level diplomat?"

"Yes, he has a culinary background. Before he became ambassador, he was a chef."

The dramatic and welcome change in nutrition at home made Mikail cut down on his old habit of patronizing restaurants all over Moscow.

One evening, when he came home from work, he asked Elena the usual question.

"What's the menu tonight, Darling?"

"Oh," she said with an alluring smile. "As an appetizer, a Bisque de Homard, followed by veal scaloppini on a bed of fettuccini, garnished with sautéed tomatoes and mushrooms. To go with it, I have selected a wonderful French red wine—a *Chateau d'Auvrais* from 1993, a very good year for red wines. For dessert I have made a Crème Brûlée."

She lit two candles and dimmed the light in the small dining room. They sat down and started eating. Then Elena raised her glass and said, "Mikail, Happy Anniversary!"

Mikail, his mouth full of veal, seemed bewildered.

"It's our first wedding anniversary, Mikail. Don't you remember?"

Embarrassed, Mikail got up from his chair, went around the table and kissed Elena. "I'm sorry, I forgot."

"Don't worry about it *this* time, but don't forget it next year, Mikail! If you do, I'll serve you sausages and mashed potatoes."

They finished their dinner in a blissful atmosphere. Leaving empty plates, forks, knives, spoons, and glasses on the table, and carrying lit candles, they retired to their bedroom.

Chapter 18

A few days after the presidential dressing down, Jerry received a telephone call from the Russian President.

"Hi, Jerry. How is everything?"

In a subdued voice, Jerry replied, "it's fine."

"Jerry, you sound a bit depressed. Is something bothering you?"

"Oh, I'm in no mood to talk about it right now."

"Sorry to hear that. Anyway, Renata and I would like to invite you to spend this coming weekend with us at our country retreat. Is that all right with you?"

"I'll be glad to come."

"Great! I'll have our driver pick you up."

- - - -

Upon his arrival at the dacha, Stanislav embraced Jerry and said, "Glad to see you again."

"Same here, Stan," Jerry said in a muted voice.

"Jerry, I'm grateful for what you have done for Elena. It may sound dramatic, but you have in fact saved her marriage. Mikail is happy as a lark with Elena's cooking and is no longer eating dinner away from home. You have restored bliss to their lives. Renata and I cannot thank you enough for what you have done for our family."

"It's no big deal. I was glad I could be of help."

Noticing Jerry's depressed mood, Stanislav said, "When I called you on the phone I sensed that something was bothering you. What's wrong?"

Shifting nervously in his chair, Jerry reluctantly uttered, "Stan, I will soon be leaving Moscow."

"Why?"

"A few days ago, while I was away from my office cooking with Elena, my State Department called the embassy about a rumored unrest in Chechnya. They were furious because they could not reach me. Then the President himself phoned me in the middle of the night raising hell about my absence from the Embassy. He informed me that I would be fired."

"Oh, come on, Jerry. The thing in Chechnya was nothing. A handful of hotheads tried to stir up some trouble. We rolled in a couple of tanks, took a few good shots, and it was all over. Tell your President this was only a minor incident, not worth bothering about!"

"But I'm sorry that you will be leaving Moscow. I didn't realize that your government was that tyrannical. It reminds me of past actions, years ago, by the former despots ruling this country with a brutal iron fist. Regardless of all that, I owe you a favor for what you have done for Elena. Is there anything I can do for you before you return to the United States?"

"Well, Stan, I hate to bring up an old matter which years ago created such ado here and in my country, but I'm still interested in Borovsky's salad dressing recipe. I wonder whether there is a way of getting it without stirring up another controversy."

"Let me think about it, Jerry. It may be something to give to my think tank. Maybe they can come up with some workable ideas."

- - - -

At home, after the weekend, Jerry pondered whether he had stepped out of bounds by getting his friend, the Russian President, involved in a potentially explosive matter. He was inclined to ask Stanislav to drop the whole thing, but then again, he thought, *why not wait and see what his advisers come up with?*

A week later, he received a phone call from the Russian President's secretary.

"Mr. Ambassador, the President would like to see you in his office. Could you come over at 3 o'clock today?"

"Yes, I'll be there," Jerry answered.

When he arrived, Stanislav greeted him with a mischievous smile.

"My think tank has come up with two alternatives. The first one goes like this: Borovsky's unproven claim that you, the American ambassador, were involved in the old salad dressing espionage affair could have hurt our friendly relations with your country. This is enough of a pretext for closing his restaurant and expelling him to Siberia, where he would not get a license to open a new restaurant unless he surrenders the recipe to my government. The second alternative would be to make Borovsky Purveyor to the President of Russia. In return for this honor, he hands over the salad dressing recipe to my administration. After considerable thought, I have decided the second solution is much more civilized. Alternative one smells too much of past strong-arm tactics by our previous governments. Clever isn't it?"

"Stan, it's brilliant!" Jerry exclaimed.

Stanislav continued, "I will handle this personally with Borovsky. We are going to make a big splash about it, with press and TV coverage. The whole country will get to know about this appointment, which I'm sure will make Borovsky very proud."

On his way back to the embassy Jerry mused, *These Russians are a cunning bunch.*

- - - -

Borovsky was in his kitchen when the telephone rang. A waiter answered the call.

"I'm the President's secretary," a lady said. "Could I talk to Mr. Borovsky?"

"Just a moment I'll get him. He is in the kitchen." The waiter rushed into the kitchen. "Mr. Borovsky, a lady from the Kremlin is on the line. She wants to talk to you!"

Borovsky took the receiver. "I'm Jaroslav Borovsky. What can I do for you Madam?"

"The President would like to see you next Wednesday at his office at 3 o'clock in the afternoon. Is this convenient for you?"

"Certainly, Madam. I'll be there."

Why would the President see me? Borovsky asked himself. *Maybe the Kremlin has a catering job for me. That would be great!*

Chapter 19

On the day of his appointment with the President, Borovsky arrived at the Kremlin. He saw several vans from radio and TV stations parked near the entrance to the presidential offices. Led by a government official he was steered to a large ornate hall adjacent to the presidential suite. When he entered, the place was full of media people. The President emerged from a side door.

"Welcome to the Kremlin, Mr. Borovsky. I was impressed when your restaurant was honored with the Restaurant of the Year award. You ought to be mighty proud of that achievement."

"Yes, I am, Mr. President."

"Mr. Borovsky, as I understand it, your *Salad a la Kremlin* was one of the major reasons for your selection. And, of course, everybody knows that the secret of a good salad mainly lies in its dressing."

"Yes, that's true, Mr. President."

"Several foreign dignitaries and diplomats have eaten in your restaurant and they all rave about your salad dish. Here at the Kremlin we have, as you can well imagine, a lot of entertainment. We host many parties and our cooks are always looking for ways to expand and improve the menus for the benefit of our many guests. Therefore, I would like our chefs to add to their selection of condiments *your* salad dressing. When you provide us with the recipe, I will appoint you Presidential Purveyor."

"I'm deeply honored, Mr. President. I will be glad to provide your office with the recipe for the dressing, and I thank you so much for the appointment."

Then the President presented Borovsky with a gold-framed proclamation of the appointment. With scores of cameras running and clicking, Borovsky took a bow when he was handed the official document.

The President continued, "Mr. Borovsky, you have the right to use this presidential appointment for promotion of your business in any way you wish. Should you at a later date decide to start a factory for mass-production of your salad dressing for nationwide distribution you can, of course, include this recognition on your labels, and should you need start-up financing, I'm sure we can be of help."

"Thank you, Mr. President!" Borovsky exclaimed.

They shook hands, and when Borovsky left the Kremlin, reporters crowded around him for interviews.

- - - -

The next morning a presidential aide picked up the recipe at Borovsky's restaurant. A few days later Jerry received a call from the Russian President.

"Jerry, I've got the recipe!"

"Terrific! Thank you Stan!"

An envelope containing details of the recipe translated into English was delivered to Jerry at the embassy. He opened it and noticed the list included coskev, a Russian herb. All the other ingredients were available back home. Jerry immediately went to a supermarket and bought a good supply of the herb.

When Jerry's departure was drawing near, the Kremlin organized a big farewell party for him. Senior government officials led by the President, along with the entire diplomatic corps were present at the formal dinner. Jerry studied the menu card on the table. It included as appetizer, *Salad a la Kremlin*. When it was time for dessert and coffee, the Russian President, glass in hand, rose and spoke.

"Ladies and Gentlemen. It is with a sense of sadness that we learn that His Excellency, Jerry Sweikert, the American ambassador will soon be leaving us. During his tenure in Moscow, he has very ably represented his country's best interests, and his presence here has greatly contributed to strengthening the friendly relations between the United States and my country. While my government and I will miss the pleasant and constructive interaction with His Excellency, we wish him all the best as he returns home. Therefore, ladies and gentlemen, let us raise our glasses in a heartfelt farewell salute to this outstanding American."

Jerry, visibly touched, took in the wave of applause from the audience. He shook the President's hand and said, "Thank you, Stan, for everything."

"Jerry, don't mention it!"

- - - -

The day before his departure from Moscow, Jerry went to Restaurant Borovsky to have lunch. When he entered, he noticed a framed proclamation, *Presidential Purveyor* signed by the Russian President hanging over the reception desk. He sat down and ordered a *Salad a la Kremlin*. The waiter brought him the salad on a plate adorned with the presidential seal. Borovsky happened to be in the restaurant area. When he saw Jerry, he approached his table and asked, "Sir, haven't we met before?"

"Yes, years ago!" Jerry smirked.

"Were you not the American gentleman who asked me for the salad dressing recipe?"

"Yes, that was me, and I got it!"

Bewildered, Borovsky asked, "How did you get it?"

"From a friend of mine." Then pausing for a moment he added with a grin, "It's amazing what a little coskev can do to a salad dressing."

THE END

ATHENA'S DISCIPLES

Chapter 1

Throughout the years, they had met each day at four in the afternoon. Their usual haunt was a very old café—Hviid's Wine Room in Copenhagen, the capital of Denmark.

In 1723, an illustrious innkeeper, Ernst Hviid, opened the café to cater to the sophisticated wine-drinking class. Since then, through a succession of owners, the average person found it to be a haven of sorts.

The consumption of wine and other liquor lost ground to beer, the predominant beverage in the café. It had not changed much since it was opened. The low ceiling was still there, and the old dark wooden wall panels were original. The slanted and uneven floor remained, and the chairs and tables showed traces of centuries of wear and tear. The walls were covered with small, old framed engravings and the dimmed lights inside created a cozy atmosphere.

The old café was located at King's Square, in the heart of the city. It was a preferred hangout for actors, ballet dancers and other members of the art community such as painters and writers. Business people and politicians could also be spotted in this well-known watering hole. It was a place of barter, as well, and it was a common sight to see a needy artist in paint-spotted clothes trading artwork for beer.

The members of the group were graduate students working on their masters degrees at the University of Copenhagen. There were five of them. Because of their activism and visibility around campus, they were known as the *Gang of Five*. Over bottles of beer and under clouds of cigarette smoke, their animated discussions covered a wide range of topics from their girlfriends to politics. They were all bright and very articulate students at the top of their classes. Although they came from very diverse family backgrounds, they had become very close friends since entering university as freshmen.

John, a tall and handsome ladies man, was the leader of the group. He was a mainstay at many wild beer-splashing student parties. His major was Political Science and he came from a wealthy family. His father was president of one of the country's largest banks. His ancestors included a long line of industry leaders and politicians. Much to the chagrin of his parents, who were of a traditional conservative bent, he was a very active member of the *Youth for Socialism* organization.

Carl was of average build and wore horn-rimmed glasses. He was a Math Major. His family included a string of academics. His father was Professor of Biology at the university.

Svend had rugged features and was the brains of the group. Rather than participating in wild student parties, he preferred small group discussions on political topics. He majored in Philosophy and was a leader in the youth wing of the Socialist party. His father was a truck-lift operator and a prominent labor union leader.

Peter had a hefty build. He was a bright and articulate debater and a law student. His father was a Supreme Court Justice and his family lineage included a number of lawyers and judges. A leader in the Conservative Youth movement, he frequently clashed with the liberal-leaning members of the group whenever politics were discussed. He often fiercely contested the government's intrusion into the lives of citizens, through what he called *exaggerated social largesse*.

Erik was skinny. He was a quiet and thoughtful individual whose major was Theology. His goal was to follow in the footsteps of his father, a priest in a rural community. His hobby was collecting butterflies, which he kept neatly pinned and categorized by species and features in glass-covered boxes in his small studio apartment. A prolific writer, he was the editor of *The Owl*, the student newspaper, to which the other members of the group were active contributors.

Chapter 2

Over a period of several years, the country had developed and perfected an extensive social welfare net, whereby the government took care of its citizens from the cradle to the grave. The cost of this massive social system was defrayed through a high level of taxation. Although most of the population complained about the high levies, the vast majority had come to accept and enjoy the advantages of this social welfare system.

Successive administrations, mainly the conservative ones, traditionally opposed many of the social programs but had been reluctant to tamper with this ingrained and costly, albeit well-run, system.

University education fell under this welfare umbrella and was free-of-charge. Apart from free instruction, students are allowed to apply for, and are granted, a stipend by the government to help them with their living expenses. Students from all walks of life enjoyed this privilege. Even those from well-to-do families were eligible for this program, although the amount of aid was adjusted according to the wealth of the individual student's parents.

The Conservative party had won the recent general elections and had formed a coalition government with a few smaller fringe parties. Being traditionally against many state-sponsored and costly social programs, the new administration, faced with budgetary problems, decided to abolish the stipend for students. Although the annulment was met with stiff resistance from the opposition in the House of Representatives, the government managed by a razor-thin majority of votes to enact the law ending the much cherished aid.

The official announcement that the stipend had been revoked created a nationwide uproar among university students who protested vigorously against the measure. Many citizens who felt the new law was unfair expressed sympathy for the students. Huge student demonstrations erupted all over the country. Their leaders took to the podiums to deliver fiery speeches amid a sea of posters condemning the government's action. Burning of effigies of the Minister of Education was a common feature at these boisterous manifestations.

The press was bombarded with letters from angry readers decrying the draconian steps taken by the new administration. Newspaper editorials, showing sympathy for the students' plight, strongly condemned the annulment of the stipend. Despite the massive outpouring of support for the students' cause, the government would not budge.

- - - -

The *Gang of Five* seized upon the stipend matter to get into action. They held an emergency meeting in the old café to discuss the situation. After having ordered the usual round of beer, they began their deliberations. John opened the discussion.

"What do you fellows suggest we do? So far the general uproar about the stipend thing and the demonstrations have had no effect."

"What about organizing a nationwide strike by our fellow students and the members of the faculties?" Erik asked.

"Most students are already staying away from classes. Our professors will probably not be paid if they join a strike. Anyway, it's doubtful it would affect the situation very much. Svend, have you got any ideas?"

"We could storm into the House of Representatives when it's in session, create havoc, disrupt the proceedings and shake up the politicians there!"

"I don't think it will work," Peter injected. "The security people would probably throw us out. We might even be arrested for disorderly conduct and put in the slammer! In my opinion it won't advance our cause."

"What about a hard-hitting full-page article in the major newspapers condemning the government's action?" Erik suggested. "They would certainly agree to publish it."

"Come on Erik," Carl said. "I know you love to write, but the newspapers are already full of editorials, most of them sympathetic to our cause. It wouldn't help much."

"What about kidnapping the Minister of Education and holding him hostage?" John jokingly suggested.

Amid laughter, Peter replied, "John, it's a crime, you know. All of us would end up in jail. You're nuts!"

"Of course, I know that. I was just trying to throw some humor into our discussion. But we absolutely have to do *something* dramatic!"

"Wait," Svend said with a grin. "I like the word kidnap. I've got it. What about kidnapping the Minister of Education's bicycle, and holding it hostage until he changes his mind and reinstates the stipend? We know that he rides his bicycle to and from work each day."

"You must be kidding!" John said, "It's naïve to think the government would trade a piece of legislation for a bicycle. But I agree the action would get the matter some exposure and generate some amusement too."

"Peter, you know the law. Is kidnapping a bicycle a crime?"

Peter laughed and replied, "To kidnap a person is clearly a crime. To take possession of a bicycle and hold it for a period of time may, in my opinion, only be a misdemeanor. It may expose us to legal complications, but that's a risk we'll have to take, if we decide to go ahead with a kidnapping plan."

John turned toward Erik and said, "You will one day become a man of the cloth. You probably know more about sins than the rest of us. What is your opinion? Is it a sin to take temporary possession of a bike?"

Pausing for a moment, Erik replied. "There is nothing in the Bible dealing specifically with kidnapping of bicycles. But I think it would come pretty close to sinning. On the other hand, the Good Book clearly tells us we are all born sinners, but in the end God will forgive us if we stray."

"Well, that takes care of that," John said. "Do we all agree that kidnapping the minister's bike is the way to go?"

"Hold it!" Svend said. "Do you guys really think it would change anything if we kidnapped the minister's bike and sent him a nice letter telling him he would get it back, if the stipend is reinstated? It would give us some exposure for sure. The press would pick it up, but it would be considered just a funny prank. The government stands to economize millions by doing away with the stipend. It won't give in because we took possession of a lousy bike."

"I've got it!" Carl said. "We could try to get on national television masked like real kidnappers. We would appear with the minister's bicycle and make a statement lambasting him and the government for doing away with the stipend. We would announce that the bike would be held hostage until the stipend is reinstated. We would have a huge audience if we did that."

"You are right," John said. "Getting on TV would be great. It will give the stipend matter a lot of exposure. Assuming that a TV station would agree to put us on, it would probably be for only one appearance."

A moment of silence followed.

Erik's face lit up. "Not necessarily. We could try to get the TV station to agree that we appear on successive nightly primetime newscasts. Each time we are on, we would remove a part from the bicycle. For example, at the first TV appearance we would remove the saddle, the next the handlebars and so on. If the stipend were reinstated, we would stop the program. If against all odds we can swing it that way our exposure would be extensive and continual and this kind of segment would no doubt amuse the viewers."

"Erik, it's brilliant," John said. "I didn't realize that a budding priest like you would have that much imagination!"

"John, don't you know that God works in mysterious ways. If you study the Bible, you will find many examples of this. Sometimes he works through people, and I was fortunate it was my turn!"

"Can we all agree this is the plan?" John asked.

While downing their beers they answered in unison with a resounding, "Yes!"

"Okay," John continued. "I suggest that you, Peter, the most eloquent among us, set up a personal meeting with the Program Director of NBS to present our plan. I believe that NBS, being a non-profit government institution, may agree to give us free airtime. I don't think the two privately owned television stations would be interested."

Chapter 3

Peter met with Lars Petersen, NBS' Program Director, in his office.

"Mr. Petersen, my name is Peter. I'm a student at the University of Copenhagen, and I'm here to ask for your help. I'm sure you're familiar with the controversy surrounding the decision by the government to eliminate the student stipend and the furor it has caused."

"Yes I know about it, and I think it was a bad decision. When I was a student myself years ago, I benefited greatly from this aid. I came from a working class family, and had it not been for this stipend, I would not be sitting here in front of you today. I agree with you. The unfair measure taken by the government is a slap in the face of our country's students."

Encouraged by Petersen's positive attitude, Peter outlined the plan.

"It's innovative but rather dramatic," Petersen said. "In principle, I have an open mind to your plan. However, you realize that you fellows would probably be arrested for kidnapping the bicycle. We, at NBS, might also get into legal trouble for abetting you. On the other hand, our news programs are rather dull and could use some spice. The material we have to work with in this placid country is not particularly earthshaking.

"We're losing viewers to the two commercial TV stations. They are, as you know, supported by ad revenues enabling them to buy a variety of programs of entertaining nature. By contrast, we are hamstrung financially as we can't air ads, and we work within a very tight government budget. We're, however, always interested in showing entertaining programs, especially if they are free of charge. But your idea of getting on TV as masked kidnappers may well cross the line."

"But isn't this a matter of free speech?" Peter asked. "Which I presume a broadcast station, especially a public one, would *not* be against."

"Yes, that may be true. Give me a few days to think it over. I'll get back to you with my decision. And, by the way, call me Lars."

Chapter 4

A few days later Lars Petersen phoned Peter summoning him to his office at NBS.

"Peter, I've been giving your project some thought, and I'm prepared to allocate airtime to your group as a part of our evening prime time newscasts. It's an opportunity for us to shake up our viewers with something that's both newsworthy *and* entertaining. But, I'm also acutely aware we may run into trouble with the government, and I may be fired and the program scrapped. However, I'm prepared to take that risk. By the way, how many nightly segments are involved?"

"Well, that depends on what happens to the stipend. If this effort, along with pressures from other fronts, make the government give in, we would stop and return the minister's bicycle. But, if the authorities continue to drag their feet, or in the end refuse to retract the measure, we would continue our appearances. As I've already told you, the idea is to remove one part from the bicycle each time we get on the air until nothing is left of the bicycle."

Peter grinned and added, "As you know, Lars, there're quite a few parts on a bicycle, even a standard one—presumably the type the minister is riding. Another thing, we ask for total anonymity. Can we count on that?"

"Of course! But give us ample notice before the program is launched so the practical arrangements for the broadcasts can be in place."

"Thank you, Lars. Our group and all our nation's students will be grateful for your cooperation. And when this thing is over we would like to invite you for a beer or two at Hviid's Wine Room."

"I'll be there!"

- - - -

On his return from NBS Peter immediately assembled the group at their usual haunt. When he shared Petersen's favorable reaction with the others the spirit in the group soared. The good news was celebrated with several rounds of beer.

"Now guys," John said. "The next step is to take possession of the bicycle." Amid laughter he asked, "Who among you looks like a typical kidnapper?"

"Erik is the man for the job," Carl suggested. "He'd probably be under divine guidance and protection in carrying out this vital mission!"

"Do you agree, Erik?" John asked.

"Yes I do, so help me God!"

"When you seize the bike, bring along a new lock and install it," Sven added. "If it already has a lock, break it and replace it with the new one. Then ride the bike to an area close to the NBS complex. Park it in one of the bike racks for easy access, lock the bike, and for God's sake remember the code. After each nightly broadcast, we'll have to move the bicycle to another rack near the building. If we leave it in the same rack, night after night, it may appear abandoned, and perhaps be stolen."

Chapter 5

The next morning, before the offices at the Ministry of Education opened, Erik moved around in front of the main entrance and the nearby bicycle racks. There was a lot of traffic in the area. Government workers arrived in a steady stream, many of them by bicycle.

Finally, the minister turned up. He parked his bicycle in one of the racks, removed his attaché case from the luggage carrier and entered the building. After waiting a few minutes, Erik slowly approached the bicycle. Because of the heavy circulation of people, the risk of being observed was minimal. He was relieved to find that the bicycle had no lock. He removed it from the rack and slowly walked it out into the street, jumped on it and took off.

On his way to the broadcast building, he told John by cell phone that he had possession of the bicycle. He parked it in a rack near the NBS building, installed the new lock, and wrote down the code.

- - - -

At the end of his workday, the minister went to pick up his bicycle. To his dismay, it was gone.

"Damned thief!" he mumbled, "I wish I had a lock on it."

He walked to the nearest bus stop and boarded a bus for home. When he was near his home, his wife was in the garden and noticed him walking up the driveway.

"Alex, where is your bicycle?" she asked.

"It was stolen!"

Unable to suppress a smile, she said, "It's not too bad. It's time you get a new one anyway. I know you love that old bicycle. But don't you think it would be nice for you to get a more up-to-date model?"

"I know, Gerda, but that bicycle is of great sentimental value to me. Don't you remember years ago when we were dating? We cycled down to the lake, watching the sunset. On that beautiful summer evening in July, I proposed to you."

"Yes Alex, I remember. Your bicycle was brand new then. But sentimentalism aside, Dear, you should have replaced that old thing years ago."

"I'll wait until the spring to get a new one. The winter is approaching and until the weather is milder and more reliable, I guess I'll have to use public transportation."

Inside the house, while Gerda was preparing dinner, she brought up the stipend matter.

"I've heard on the radio and read in the newspaper about the large demonstrations by students. The stipend matter must give you and the administration a lot of headaches. In my opinion, it is unfair to take away this support from the students. We're fortunate we can afford to keep our two boys in school and help them out a little with their living expenses. But, think about those families of very modest means. What are they going to do? There must be other costs in the government's budget that could be cut with less painful effect."

"I know, Gerda. I have fought in vain against the cancellation of the stipend. The Prime Minister is a stubborn man. It was entirely his decision, and I had no choice but to follow his directives. Do you think that I, being responsible for our country's education, like it?"

Gerda resumed her preparations for the evening meal. When she looked out the window, she saw their two sons approaching the house from the street.

"Alex, we're having guests for dinner tonight. Per and Mads are honoring us with their visit! I better make more spaghetti."

Gerda and Alex greeted their sons in the doorway.

"What a surprise!" Gerda exclaimed. "We don't see much of you since you entered the university! How are you doing?"

"We're doing all right, Mads replied. "But, we thought we would stop by for a home cooked meal. Even with your help we're short of money now that the goddamned government has taken away our allowance!"

Alex cringed but kept silent. They all sat down for dinner and small talk. Alex was relieved the touchy stipend subject was not discussed. When the meal was over, the two boys left the house, each carrying boxes of cereals under the arms.

Chapter 6

The country had a single chamber parliamentary system of government. The ministers in charge of the various departments were also common members of the House of Representatives and were present at all sessions. The daily running of the departments was the responsibility of directors, who were career civil servants of no particular political leaning, at least not during office hours.

The stipend matter continued to be a hot political potato for the government. The Prime Minister and the Minister of Education were relentlessly attacked by the opposition whenever the House was in session. And angry outbursts on each side of the aisle shook the venerable old House. The attempts by the Speaker to calm the situation were often futile.

Large groups of noisy students, occupying the spectator's gallery at every session, waived large protest posters and showered the assembled politicians with catcalls to disrupt the proceedings. When the Speaker, furiously hammering his gavel on the lectern, failed to restore order, the students were physically removed from the gallery.

- - - -

In the meantime, the practical arrangements for the kidnappers' appearance on TV had been completed. They were now ready to go on the air for the first time.

In the evening, after the news of current events had been broadcast, the TV anchorman made the following announcement:

"Tonight we have a special news segment."

The *Gang of Five* entered and sat down facing TV viewers. Wearing masks, they held up the minister's bicycle above a table in front of them. Then the following pre-recorded message was broadcast:

"This is a message for the Minister of Education. Your decision to abolish the stipend for our country's needy students is a disgrace. It amounts to nothing less than government tyranny, and will not be tolerated by our nation's student community. It puts many of our fellow students in a very difficult financial situation.

"Until this unfair measure is reversed, your bicycle, shown here, will remain in our custody. During successive broadcasts, we will gradually dismantle it, part by part, unless you and the government come to your senses and restore the stipend.

"To commute to and from your office, you will now have to use public transportation. As we don't want you to be out of pocket, we have mailed to your office a coupon book with tickets. Tonight we'll start by removing the saddle and we'll appear on the air regularly, if need be, until nothing is left of your bicycle. Good night, Sir."

With that, one of the kidnappers held up a wrench and removed the saddle.

- - - -

The night of the broadcast, the minister had settled down into his favorite chair at home to watch the evening news. When the segment with the kidnappers appeared, he yelled to his wife who was working in the kitchen.

"Gerda, come in here quickly!" Pointing at the TV screen, he said, "That is my bicycle, and those masked thugs stole it!"

"Alex, they have only taken temporary possession of your bike and you will get it back one day! But, to be frank with you, I hope they keep it forever. I told you before it should be replaced!"

When the broadcast was over, Alex spoke. "Gerda, my bicycle has been cleaned. It looks like new now. I really miss it!"

"It's really a paradox Alex," she said with a smile. "That old thing has now become a media star! You ought to be mighty proud. Your old bicycle has achieved prominence!"

"It's not funny, Gerda!"

"Come on Alex! I thought the thing was quite funny!"

Chapter 7

The following evening the group appeared again as part of the news broadcast with the following message:

"Mr. Minister, we know you're missing your dear old bicycle. We're deeply sorry to prevent you from getting your daily exercise bicycling to and from work. But, be assured, your bike is in good hands with us and we'll take great care of it. It was somewhat dirty when we took it. We have cleaned it well, oiled it and put on a brand new lock for its security. And, when the stipend matter has been resolved to our satisfaction, we'll replace the worn tires with new ones and have the bicycle serviced before we return it to you.

"In the meantime, much to our regret, we now have to remove the handlebars. It's our sincere hope we will one day soon cease cannibalizing your bicycle. But, that depends on what happens to the stipend. Good night, Sir!"

- - - -

The news item now referred to by the TV anchor as the *Minister's Bicycle*, caught on, became very popular and caused lots of laughter among viewers. Although the country was a bastion of liberalism and free speech, most viewers were surprised the kidnappers had not already been arrested, and that the national TV station was willing to broadcast this kind of controversial news item.

An increasing number of viewers, always looking for entertainment, were now eagerly awaiting the next installment of the *Minister's Bicycle*. The huge interest generated throughout the country by this very popular program made thousands of viewers switch from the commercial TV stations to NBS, and its ratings soared. The executives at the two independent channels were scratching their heads, seeing their former high ratings taking a nosedive.

The people at NBS were thrilled about the success of the popular news item, especially Lars Petersen, who had gone out on a limb in authorizing the project. He liked the fact that even a standard bicycle has many parts.

- - - -

The third night, the kidnappers came on with the following statement:

"Mr. Minister, we, *Disciples of Athena*, the Goddess of Wisdom, admire those people who don't choose to attend our institutions of higher learning. Those who toil each day with their hands, drive our trains and buses, build and repair our roads. Those who work in our shops and wait on us in restaurants. These, and many others, are the backbone of our society.

"But while we salute these fellow citizens, it's equally important for our nation to continue developing a strong cadre of professionals with academic backgrounds in this increasingly complicated, interconnected, and competitive world. Therefore, it's vital that young people from all walks of life, regardless of their families' economic means, have access to our universities.

"Unfortunately, Mr. Minister, the edict to stop government support will prevent many of these young men and women from realizing their dreams of a university education. Our nation should not foster an academic upper class based on the financial ability of parents to send their children to the university. Tonight, alas, we will remove the tires on your bicycle. Good night, Sir."

Chapter 8

The *Minister's Bicycle* newscasts lent impetus to the ongoing upheaval in the House of Representatives about the stipend matter and the constant calls by the opposition for the government to resign. The Prime Minister was furious, and during one of the sessions, amid a loud chorus of jeers, he mounted the podium in the chamber.

"Our nation is faced with possible anarchy because of the stipend situation. But, my government will not give in to a bunch of deranged students. And it's completely unacceptable that our public TV station allows a group of rabble-rousers to appear on the air with their mudslinging!"

He turned toward the Minister of Justice, and angrily asked, "Kai, isn't it a crime for someone to seize property belonging to somebody else? Also, can't we put a stop to that nonsense on TV? Isn't it an illegal use of a state institution?"

"Niels, seizing the bicycle is clearly a felony. The students' action amounts to extortion. As for the broadcast, some may consider them to be expressions of free speech. We *could* ask Professor Carstens, the respected expert in constitutional law at the university, for his opinion."

"Contact this so-called expert immediately so we can clear up this matter!"

The Leader of the Opposition stepped up to the podium to speak.

"Trying to shut down the students' TV broadcast is pure hogwash. Where would we be as a nation today, if in the past, we had tyrannically suppressed the freedom to speak out—even on controversial issues? When this administration seeks a ruling from Professor Carstens, I predict it will end up with egg on its face!"

He sat down, amid applause from the opposition and the spectator's gallery and repeated calls for the government to resign.

Professor Carstens was of the opinion that the broadcasts by the group were legal expressions of free speech. The ministers in the cabinet discussed whether the students should be arrested, but decided it was politically expedient not to do so.

- - - -

For the fourth broadcast the kidnappers brought along a young female student. She addressed the TV audience:

"My name is Caroline. I'm a student at the University of Copenhagen and my major is Biology. My dream after graduation is to work as a scientist in a lab. I love animals, especially small white mice. To see these creatures having fun pedaling on a spinning wheel is a pure delight to the eye. These tiny mice are important elements in the research to find new cures for many diseases. The study of the interaction of these little rodents can be a valuable research tool for insight into human behavior as well.

"In short, working with these small mice and other kinds of animals in the interest of science is vital for the well-being of our nation's people. I come from a working class background. My father has been laid off from work. He is a garbage collector and my mother does domestic cleaning—three houses a day. Because they are running out of money, my parents have told me they were unable to keep me in the university any longer. So, my dreams of one day working in a lab with white mice are now going up in smoke. I'll probably have to study house cleaning, and become a sidekick to my mother."

When she had left the studio, Peter said, "There you have it, Mr. Minister. Here's a bright young woman whose dreams have been shattered by the action taken by you and the government. What a waste of brainpower. In honor of this young student, we shall proceed with the removal of the pump from your bicycle. Good night, Sir."

Peter took off the pump, and when the TV anchor returned to the other news items, he couldn't suppress a smile, and loud roars of laughter coming from the broadcast control room could be heard by the viewers.

- - - -

Peter's parents, the Supreme Court judge and his wife, had been watching the news broadcast that evening. While he was puffing on a

84

cigar, she put down her knitting work, turned toward him and remarked, "Alfred, don't you think the kidnapping thing on TV was quite entertaining?"

"Yes Dear, I do! But, the government is up in arms about the students' broadcasts and wanted to stop them. They checked with Professor Carstens to determine whether the programs were lawful. His opinion was they were permissive examples of free speech, and between you and me, he's right. On the other hand, the young fellows have clearly committed a felony by seizing the bicycle. They will probably be arrested, and that will be the end of the *Minister's Bicycle* program."

"That's too bad! By the way, I noticed the voice of the speaker this evening sounded much like Peter's. Do you think he's involved?"

"I don't know for sure. But, you're right. It resembled his voice, and strictly between us, if he's part of the group, we ought to be proud of him."

Chapter 9

The popularity of the *Minister's Bicycle* news item, the opinion by Professor Carstens in favor of the kidnappers, and the tumultuous scenes in the House of Representatives, added stimulus to the student demonstrations. They were now in overdrive. More and more students boycotted classes. Faculty members joined the sea of angry protesters, and the universities shut down. Police on horseback were called in, and swinging their clubs over the heads of the protesters, they tried with limited success to get a handle on the rallies as they grew larger and larger.

Amid the chaos, the kidnappers continued their TV appearances, and on the fifth night, they appeared with the following message:

"Mr. Minister, don't you and the government realize that all the havoc caused by your decision to abolish the stipend is bringing our proud nation to its knees, preventing a normal and orderly governance of our country? Are you and your cohorts in the administration blind to the real possibility that the government may fall, and you will be out of a job? For our country to lose such a dedicated civil servant like you would be a shame.

"It's very simple. Just reverse the edict, reinstate the stipend, and we students will happily return to our classrooms. But, as long as you and your colleagues remain obstinate, we will continue our nightly broadcasts. There are still many parts left on your bicycle and that will keep us on the air. Tonight we'll dismantle the chain. Good night, Sir."

At the end of the address, one of the kidnappers removed the chain, and Carl added, "Here goes the chain. What a pity, it's just been cleaned and oiled!"

- - - -

John called a meeting at the café to review the progress made so far. The spirits were high among the group and, as usual, an array of beer bottles covered nearly every inch of their table.

"Things are going well," he said. "We're getting our message across, but we must think of new twists in our presentations to keep up the momentum. The impact of our TV appearances depends on our ability to continue them with innovation and bite, spiced with humor. They must not become stale. We must create new material for the upcoming segments. I'm afraid we'll have to skip a few nights, until we've new ammunition. So come on boys, let's have some new ideas!"

"What we *could* do next time is to invite the Prime Minister to argue the government's case," Peter suggested. "It would be very democratic to provide him with a forum. To present both sides of an argument is always a sound principle, and it would no doubt sit well with the TV audience and create respect for us as being fair-minded."

"You talk like a goddamned lawyer!" Carl replied with a broad grin. "We know, one day you will be one of those long-winded attorneys whose legalistic lingo is mostly bullshit!"

"For once," Erik said, "I think our esteemed legal scholar is right. In my opinion, his suggestion to invite the Prime Minister to participate in the fun is terrific. However, I'm afraid the august civil servant, having had it with us, would excuse himself. But we should at least try to get him onboard."

It was decided that Peter should compose a letter from the kidnappers to be sent to the Prime Minister's office, with an RSVP to the bartender in Hviid's Wine Room.

Chapter 10

A few days later, a brief reply headlined: *"To Whom It May Concern"*, was received by the bartender who handed it to the Gang *of Five*. It was signed by the Prime Minister's personal secretary. It read:

The Prime Minister acknowledges receipt of your letter, but regrets to inform you that due to other pressing commitments he is unable to respond positively to your invitation.

"It was expected," Erik said. "His Excellency wouldn't have the guts to enter the lion's den. But, what about lining up some other dope who agrees with the government's decision—a person of prominence? I think Frederik Seefelt, the well-respected economist who wrote the book on economics used at the university, would be an ideal candidate. We know from his editorials in the press that he sides with the government."

"Great idea," Carl replied. "We should arrange with NBS that the TV anchor prefaces the next segment by telling the audience that we have tried in vain to invite the Prime Minister to take part in the broadcast. As for the economist, we should ask the TV station to invite him to appear on the program instead. Do we all agree?"

They all nodded, and John added, "Let's get the economist in the hot seat."

- - - -

When it was ready to be broadcast, the TV anchorman made the following announcement:

"As part of the news tonight, the kidnappers had invited the Prime Minister to participate in the *Minister's Bicycle* segment, but he declined. We, at NBS, called instead upon the well-known economist, Frederik Seefelt, to make a presentation."

The economist appeared and sat down at a table in front of the kidnappers. Facing the cameras, he began.

"Good Evening. I am glad to have the opportunity to explain the background for the government's decision to eliminate certain items in its budget. I, too, regret that the popular financial aid to our university students has been cut. Believe me, our student community has not been singled out. Several other expenditures in the national budget have, out of sheer necessity, been reduced or even eliminated. Our country is currently facing severe budgetary problems. Because of the present sluggish economy, not only in our country, but all over Europe, our government has been compelled to tighten its belt.

"Our exports, which have traditionally been one of the main pillars in our economy, have dropped to an uncomfortably low level. This has affected our productivity negatively. As a result, our unemployment is creeping up. Faced with these unfavorable circumstances the government cannot generate enough revenues through taxation to bring its budget in balance. Therefore, it is reasonable that our student community must, like other segments of our society, bear its share of the burden during these difficult times.

"Until the economy turns around, I would suggest that more students seek part-time employment to defray all or part of their living expenses. It is my fervent hope that over time our economy will recover sufficiently to allow for the reinstatement of the stipend to our students. Good night and thank you for listening."

Svend stood up and turned toward the economist. "Mr. Seefelt, we appreciate your thoughtful presentation. However, allow me to point out, for the record, that many of us already work. We collect old newspapers and empty bottles and cans for recycling. We walk dogs, flip hamburgers, mow lawns, babysit and do many other odd jobs. I hope you realize that we are indeed making a valuable contribution to our sagging economy, unfortunately, at the expense of our studies."

When the economist left, one of the kidnappers removed the cat eye from the bicycle.

Chapter 11

At the next meeting, the discussion among the group once again centered around new ideas to keep up the pressure on the government. However, they now realized it was time-consuming to work out the programs with sufficient variations. As a result, they had to delay the sixth installment. That did not sit well with the huge TV audience, who had come to expect to see each evening the popular news item.

The following day, NBS was bombarded with complaints from thousands of viewers. Lars Petersen was very concerned about the likely adverse impact on his station's current high rankings, and phoned John.

"John, we are getting a lot of flak from viewers. They are upset because your program was not on last night. I stuck my neck out by putting you on our prime time newscast. Don't let me down! We don't want to see our ratings drop. You must continue this thing unabated!"

"Lars, this was our thinking all along. But, we cannot just come on each time with minor changes in our message and format. We have to develop new twists in our approach, and that takes time. If not, our programs could easily become flat, and not only diminish the impact on the government, but on the TV viewers as well. Therefore, we'd suggest from now on, we appear only every second night. This would give us more time to think up new ideas. You will no doubt agree by spreading out this thing a little, it won't become routine, and the viewers will have something to look forward to, if you know what I mean."

"John, I see your point. We'll have our anchorman announce that in the future, the *Minister's Bicycle* will only be aired every other night."

- - - -

John shared with the group his conversation with Lars Petersen. "Lars is scared stiff that NBS' ratings will drop unless we keep this thing going with a minimum of disruptions. I proposed we come on every second night, and he agreed. Now we have more time to get our programs right. So guys, let's have some ideas. Don't hold back! What about you, Carl, have you got something up your sleeve?"

"Yes, what about including Freddy Clown in one of the programs? Circus Benneweis has just finished its shows here. It would be great to put him on. We could provide him with one-liners. Make him, in a funny way, ridicule the government. Another alternative would be to get one of our best-known standup comedians to dish out jokes about the stipend thing!"

"Come on, Carl, you are nuts!" Erik said. "Hasn't it dawned on you that our cause is a serious one? To have some clown or comedian turn this into a farce cheapens our message. The TV audience would certainly enjoy it, but it would dilute the thrust of what we want to convey. Sorry, old boy, it's a lousy idea. We must walk a fine line between being serious and entertaining."

"Fellows, I've got an idea," Peter said. "What about putting on a skit involving a malnourished student and a doctor? It goes like this: A skinny student in ragged clothes sees his doctor because he's feeling weak and tired. It's obvious the condition of the poor fellow is a direct result of lack of food. We could get the university's drama department to help us with this project. In your philosophy class, Svend, there's that tall, skinny and ragged-looking guy. I think his name is Ole. Don't you think he'd be ideal for the skit? He always looks depressed when I see him around campus."

"Absolutely, and for the role of the doctor we could pick Robert. He's the heavy-set little guy, who is actually studying medicine. Regarding the script for the dialogue, I suggest Erik writes it in consultation with the doctor."

Erik met with the professor in charge of the drama department and the two actors. Ole and Robert agreed to do the skit, and were told they would appear in a couple of days during the eighth TV news broadcast.

91

Chapter 12

At the seventh TV appearance, Carl started the segment on the broadcast with the following remarks:

"Mr. Minister, if you think for a moment that we're running out of gas—or more appropriately, bicycle parts—in pressing the stipend issue, you are dead wrong! Although your bike has already lost a lot of pedal power, don't worry, we've plenty of ammunition left in our tool bag. As we've told you before, we'll continue these broadcasts to the bitter end. There are still some parts left on your bicycle, although as you can clearly see now, it's no longer operational.

"It's amazing that you and the government haven't got the message. Student rallies are getting bigger and bigger, and I hope you understand that the majority of the population now stands squarely behind us. If the government falls because of the stipend matters or other issues, we'll have new elections, and the voters will certainly remember the stubborn stance by you and the government regarding the financial aid to students. We hate to do it, but tonight we'll remove the front wheel. Good night, Mr. Minister."

- - - -

All classes and lectures had come to a standstill because of the student demonstrations and the general chaos. Consequently, many students had to do their best to continue their education through self-study as they flocked to the university libraries.

John was no exception. One morning, while at the library scanning a tome on the Russian Revolution, he noticed a pretty blonde at the end of a long table. Although contacts and talking in the library were taboo, he got up and approached the young female student. She was surrounded by stacks of law books.

He whispered to her. "I see you're busy plowing though those dusty old law books. I guess you want to become a lawyer one day."

"Yes," she whispered back. "But you know, we're not supposed to talk in this place."

"I know. Therefore, shouldn't we get the hell out of here and go somewhere for a chat and a couple of beers?"

She looked up at him with an air of disdain. "You come on very strong, don't you? We don't even know each other."

"True," he replied. "But people have to meet for the first time to get acquainted."

"I still have to study for at least another hour or so before I can leave. Then I will decide whether to join you or not. By the way, I don't drink alcohol."

The young woman continued studying and John returned to his seat and pretended to read.

After an hour had passed, John looked at his watch. The young woman was taking her time finishing her reading.

After nearly two hours, John saw her close the books and slowly put them back on the shelves. He got up and went over to her again.

"Are you ready to leave now?" he asked.

"Yes," she answered in a nonchalant voice without looking at him.

When they were out in the street, he asked, "What's your name?"

"Liz Linnet," she answered.

"I'm John Hartell. Where would you like to go, Liz?"

"I really don't care. You pick the place."

"Well, if it's okay with you, I suggest we go to Hviid's Wine Room. It's my favorite hangout."

"I don't know that place," was her terse reply. "Does this place serve drinks other than alcohol?"

"Oh yes, you can get all kinds of soft drinks there."

"All right then, but I can't stay very long."

They arrived at the café. When inside, John gallantly took off Liz's coat and hung it in the coat closet. They sat down.

"What would you like to drink Liz?"

"Lemonade."

John called the waiter. "Harry, the young lady would like lemonade."

"I'm sorry, John, we don't have any lemonade, but we do have Coke and Pepsi."

"I'll take a Pepsi," Liz said.

"And you, John, the usual?" the waiter asked.

"No, give me a Pepsi too," John said.

Surprised, the waiter hesitated for a moment. Then he said, "I'll be right back with your Pepsis!"

"Liz," John asked, "Are you related to the Prime Minister, Niels Linnet?"

"Yes, I am. He is my father."

John took a big swig of his Pepsi wishing it had been a beer instead.

"I see," he said taking another gulp of his Pepsi. "What do you plan to do with your law degree once you graduate?"

"Work in labor relations."

"You mean, working on behalf of the unions?"

"Not exactly. My goal is to join a law firm specializing in labor relations. I mean one that handles conflicts between labor and management. I believe many disputes can be solved through give-and-take negotiations between the two parties. For example, strikes by workers and lock-outs by management are not viable approaches to solving problems." She paused to take a sip of her soft drink. "Well, enough about me, what is your major, John?"

"Political Science."

"I see," she said, suppressing a smile. "What are you going to use it for? It's not a particularly employable degree, unless you intend to become a civil servant, career diplomat or professor at some university."

"I know Liz, but I've always been interested in politics. Maybe I'll end up one day as a politician. Who knows?"

"I hope you realize that before you can enter politics you must have a job. Also, bear in mind that politics is often a dirty game. Believe me, I know from personal experience, in my own family. My father had to claw his way to the top, and it was ugly at times."

"What do you think about the present dilemma surrounding the stipend?"

"It's a crazy situation! Both sides are displaying a lot of stubbornness. As I told you, disputes can only be solved through good faith negotiations. I understand the government is strapped for cash because of the present dire economic climate. However, a solution to the stalemate could take the form of a stipend loan, at no interest, to be paid back to the government by the students in installments over a period of years."

"Have you ever suggested that to your father?"

"No. Since my father entered politics, we've had a strict rule at home, never to discuss or express opinions about political topics. It's a good principle never to talk about politics with family and friends. However, it amazes me that none of the so-called brains in the Administration and House of Representatives have thought about some sort of loan arrangement. However, my father would probably not agree to this. He is by nature inflexible with very strong convictions bordering on stubbornness." She picked up her purse. "Well John, I have to run now. Thanks for the drink."

"Do you think we could get together again?" John asked.

"Yes maybe, but as classes and lectures have stopped, I've got to spend a lot of time in the library. I'm usually there each morning from around eight o'clock until noon. We might run into each other then."

"I look forward to seeing you there," he said.

John helped Liz with her coat, they shook hands, and she left the café.

When she was gone, John called the waiter. "A beer please, and hurry up, Harry. I'm thirsty after that Pepsi shit!"

John met Liz every day in the library pretending to be studying. When she was ready to leave, they went to the café. Both of them kept ordering Pepsis. When she left he rinsed with beer. Little by little, their relationship grew intense. They enjoyed each other's company and eventually became more than just friends.

Chapter 13

In the meantime, the students were ready to launch the eighth installment of the *Minister's Bicycle*. NBS' make-up department had worked hard to make the malnourished student look very pale and sickly.

The segment started with remarks by Peter. "Good Evening. Tonight we'll present an example of what's likely to happen to many students in this country."

The doctor entered and sat down at a table in front of kidnappers. The student stepped in. He was tall, skinny and looked very pale. He wore old sneakers without laces and his hair was a mess.

"Young man, you don't look well. What's the problem?" asked the doctor.

"Doc, I feel sick, tired and hungry."

"When did you have your last meal?"

"Yesterday morning. It wasn't really a meal. I just had fries at McDonalds. I couldn't afford the burger."

"What are you doing to support yourself? Don't you have a job?"

"No, Doc. I'm a university student," he replied meekly.

"But don't you get some financial aid from the government to help you with your living expenses?"

"In the past, yes," he muttered. "But not now. They stopped the stipend a few months ago."

"But can't your parents help you financially?"

"No, my father was laid off from work and my mother can't work, she's an invalid—she was hit by a car."

"Where do you live?"

"I used to share a tiny room with another student, but the landlord kicked us out because we couldn't pay the rent anymore."

"Where do you live now?"

"In a homeless shelter."

"Don't they feed you there?"

"Yes, I've eaten there a few times, but they often run out of food. Many students like me go there to get a meal. Sometimes the shelter becomes so overburdened that there's not enough food for us and the shelter's other patrons."

"But is there no way for you to make some money?" asked the doctor.

"I've been able to scrape together a *little* money by picking up empty glass and plastic bottles and cans from trash containers. But one is up against strong competition for the stuff from other students, vagrants and the city's garbage collectors."

"Young man, remove your shirt so I can examine you."

Then the doctor placed his stethoscope on the chest of the student, moved it around while listening intensively.

"Take a deep breath and hold it. Now turn around so I can check your lungs."

He removed the stethoscope and in a serious voice he said, "I detect a slight palpitation of your heart. You have an irregular heartbeat. I also notice some livid spots on your skin—an early sign of scurvy due to lack of vitamin C. Young man, lack of proper nutrition is the root of many physical and mental ailments. Like the body, the brain has to be fed as well, and being a student, it's important for you that your mental faculties are not impaired!"

The doctor pulled out a banknote from his wallet, handed it to the student, and said, "Here, go and get yourself a decent meal."

"Thank you, Doc," the scrawny kid replied.

After they left the studio Peter said, "There is a real danger that what you just saw may very well become commonplace for many students suffering from malnutrition. This problem will cause overcrowding of our medical facilities. Under our free healthcare system, the afflicted students seeking treatment will be a heavy burden on our country's medical and financial resources. In the end, the huge additional costs will have to be borne by our population, either in the form of increased taxes or cuts in other vital social services.

"The increase in medical expenditures will far exceed the costs of the student stipend. It's bad economics! What's even scarier is the adverse effect on the mental capacities of our students. In this increasingly complicated and competitive world, strong brainpower is absolutely crucial for the well-being of our nation. Tonight, Mr. Minister, we'll remove the rear wheel of your bicycle as a token of sympathy for the malnourished student you just saw. Good night, Sir."

Like hundreds of thousands of viewers, the Minister of Education had been glued to the TV set each time the kidnappers came on the air. After the latest segment featuring the malnourished student, he turned toward his wife.

"Gerda, these damned students exaggerated the situation. I know we're facing a dilemma, but this thing is getting completely out of hand. The program is now being broadcast all over Europe. In fact, my German counterpart told me it has even been sub-titled in German! It reflects badly on our educational system, which is considered one of the best in Europe."

"Yes, Alex, it's a mess. In my opinion, the students have a point. You fellows running the country ought to do something to get us out of this quagmire."

"I know Gerda, for me personally, it's a disaster. As head of public instruction, it pains me to see our much admired higher education system disintegrate. I'm trying to find a solution, but my hands are tied. This matter comes up every time we meet with the Prime Minister, but he is absolutely bent on not yielding to the students. A few of the smaller parties in our coalition are now getting cold feet because of the stipend matter and at some point may well withdraw their support of the government."

"What happens then?"

"If they switch positions and side with the opposition, the government is likely to fall on a non-confidence vote in the House, unless the Prime Minister changes his mind. Then, according to our Constitution, the leaders of the various parties will be called to a conference with the Queen. She will instruct the party leaders to form a caretaker administration until new elections can be held. And there is no doubt the interim government will be dominated by the opposition."

"I guess you'll be out of a job if new elections are held and the government is defeated?"

"Yes, but I could possibly be re-elected later on as a member of the House of Representatives from my district, although any challenger would certainly hold the stipend mess against me!"

"And you may lose?"

"Yes, but with my pension and our savings, we'll be fine financially, and I'll finally get time to take care of our garden which is a mess right now!" Then he added with a tinge of humor, "And I may get my old bicycle back! By the way, Gerda, have we got any aspirin left?"

"Yes, Dear, I always keep a good supply for you!"

Chapter 14

The relationship between Liz and John had turned into a full-fledged love affair, and they met every day at the library. They frequently went to the movies, always sitting on the last row holding hands, kissing and caressing each other.

John treated Liz to cozy dinners and over lit candles, they exchanged amorous glances.

One evening Liz told John, "I've told my parents about you. They would like to invite both of us for dinner at their house. Would you like to come?"

"Sure Liz. I would be delighted to meet your parents."

"Great, I'll ask them to fix a date. They're okay. You will no doubt have a good time with them."

John reached across the table, took her hand and said, "Liz, the sparkles in your eyes compete successfully with the bright light of the candles on our table!"

"Oh come on John, you're too poetic. You embarrass me!"

He leaned over the table, kissed her, and said, "I'm a lucky guy to have met you."

- - - -

John had not shared his relationship with Liz with the group. He felt now was the time to do so. At the next regular planning meeting, he told his friends.

"I've something I want to tell you. It's a bombshell! But let's first have a round of beer." He called the waiter. "Five beers please."

"So John, what is it you want to tell us?" the others asked almost with one voice.

"I'm in love."

"So what," Carl said. "It happens to all of us from time to time."

"Yes, but the girl, Liz Linnet, is the Prime Minister's daughter."

"You must be out of your mind!" exclaimed Svend. "You're messing around with the daughter of our main antagonist! It's more than a bombshell, it's a goddamned earthquake!"

Erik cut in, and said sternly, "Don't take God's name in vain!"

"Sorry old boy. I misspoke. It's even worse than an earthquake, it's a damned tsunami!"

"I thought it was an unspoken agreement between us," Svend added, "that while we're on this important mission we should leave the ladies alone. We cannot allow unzipped pants to interfere with, and distract us from, the crusade at hand, especially when the lady is the daughter of our enemy number one! Have you lost your marbles?"

"Calm down guys," John said. "There is nothing I can do about it. Now, when I tell you her parents have invited Liz and me for dinner, you're really going to be pissed!"

"It's getting worse and worse," Peter said. "You're going to sit down for dinner with that idiot and his wife, be at your best behavior, and presumably exchange niceties with them?"

"Fellows, I assure you, it won't be controversial. If the stipend comes up, I'll speak my mind. I won't hold back!"

"I've my doubts about that," Carl injected. "Loving glances from this Liz will melt you to a point where you'll low-ball the stipend thing. Remember the old adage: *Love works in mysterious ways!*"

"Come on boys, I won't flinch!" John insisted.

After a moment of tense silence, the group began discussing the programs for the upcoming segments of the *Minister's Bicycle*.

"I've a suggestion," Erik said. "Wouldn't it be a good idea to invite the politician leading the opposition to speak as part of our program? He's with us one hundred percent. Having him throw a few punches at the administration would no doubt give our cause a shot in the arm politically. We could schedule him for the tenth segment."

There was unanimous agreement among them to extend an invitation to the politician, and Erik was selected to contact him and try to get him to appear.

Chapter 15

For the ninth episode, the group decided to come on with their own statement. Carl was assigned the task of preparing the text of the message and delivering it. After the TV anchorman had dealt with the evening's current news, Carl intoned.

"Tonight is the ninth installment in the series, the *Minister's Bicycle*, and we fear it won't be the last . . . unfortunately."

"Mr. Minister, there isn't much left of your bicycle, and that is regrettable. But, the show must go on. Do you really think we enjoy coming on TV almost every night? It's so hot in this studio with all those big lamps, but probably not quite as hot as you feel around your collar. Instead of spending lots of time and efforts on this program, we should be studying hard to get our degrees, but alas, it's not possible as long as our educational system is in shambles!

"You are the man who could get all of us out of this untenable and destructive situation. Rise up against the tyrannical powers of the Administration so we can return to the classrooms. The student community in our land would be eternally grateful for your courage in standing up for us and restoring our much-cherished educational system to normalcy. Our heartfelt thoughts go out to you, whenever we appear here. But, tonight, much to our regret, we will remove the headlight on your bicycle. Good night Sir."

- - - -

John arrived at the official residence of the Prime Minister. The house was located away from the city in a heavily wooded area near a picturesque lake. He parked his sports car on the country road out of sight of the house and walked up the long curved driveway leading up to the residence. He was met at the doorway by a maid, who led him to a wood-paneled library where he was greeted by Liz and her parents.

"Welcome, John," the Prime Minister said with a broad smile.

John shook hands with him and his wife and gave Liz a hug and a peck on the cheek.

"Young man, what would you like to drink?"

"A Pepsi, Sir," was John's response.

The maid entered the library with the drinks. The Prime Minister received a beer, his wife a glass of wine, and John and Liz the Pepsis. John glanced longingly at the beer bottle on the table.

"John," the Prime Minister said. "I understand from Liz that you're studying Political Science."

"Yes Sir. I've always been intrigued by politics especially as it relates to history—like the rise and fall of regimes and the reasons for their successes and failures. But, I'm not certain what I want to do when I graduate. I'm sure one day I'll find out. Maybe I'll enter politics."

"I see. By the way, are you related to Claus Hartell, the President of Skandia Bank?" the Prime Minister inquired.

"Yes Sir, he's my father."

"I know him very well. My government often seeks advice from him and other prominent business leaders. It's always useful for us to listen to their practical suggestions."

"I assume Sir, it may also make sense to take into account the opinions of labor."

"Yes, I suppose so. We do listen to them from time to time, although the manner in which they express their views is often strident and uncompromising."

Seeing that John had already finished his Pepsi, the Prime Minister asked, "Another Pepsi?"

Blasted drink, John thought, and suffering in silence he replied, "Yes, thank you, Sir."

The Prime Minister turned toward his daughter and asked, "Liz, how are your law studies coming along?"

"Rather well, Dad. But, due to the present stipend crisis, I now spend much more time in the library to make up for part of my studies. I certainly hope that things will soon return to normal."

"You are right. One has to make the best out of a difficult situation."

"By the way, John", he continued, "What is your opinion about the current upheaval by the students?"

"Well Sir, it's unfortunate when two sides in a dispute are unable to arrive at a mutually acceptable compromise." Liz smiled approvingly at John for his diplomatic observation.

When the maid announced that dinner was ready, they all proceeded to the formal dining room. They sat down at a long table decorated with fall flower arrangements and lit candles.

"John," Mrs. Linnet asked, "What would you like to drink with your dinner? We have some excellent white and red wines."

Unable to stand another Pepsi, he answered, "Is it possible to have a beer?"

"Yes, of course!"

The dinner was excellent—shrimp cocktail as an appetizer followed by lamb chops. Strawberries with cream rounded off the meal. After dinner, they all settled down in the library for coffee and drinks.

Thank God, the stipend matter hasn't come up again, John thought to himself.

However, his hopes were shattered when the Prime Minister said, "John, to get back to my earlier question about the student unrest, tell me your personal opinion about the stipend matter?"

"Sir, the elimination of the financial aid to students doesn't affect me. My parents are able to keep me in school. But, there are tens of thousands of students who are less fortunate than I. For many of them and their families, the lack of this support places a heavy financial burden on them."

There was no further discussion on the subject. At the end of the evening, John and Liz walked down, hand in hand, to his car and took off. After having kissed her good night and dropping her off at her apartment, he continued on to Hviid's Wine Room for a much-needed beer.

Chapter 16

The following afternoon, John met as usual with his friends in the café. The four of them were anxious to know how the dinner with the Prime Minister went. Svend led off the questioning.

"John, did you have a good time last night?" he asked.

"Yes, it was a pleasant evening. I think it went very well. The dinner was excellent."

"Did the stipend matter come up?"

"Yes, initially in a kind of indirect way. The Prime Minister asked my opinion about the student unrest."

"What did you answer?"

"As I wanted to avoid a long delicate discussion, I simply told him it was unfortunate when two sides in a dispute couldn't find mutual ground."

"I knew it," Carl added. "Because you probably wanted to be in the good book of this Liz, you gave a wishy-washy reply and skirted the subject. You acted like a chicken. You should have hammered the S.O.B. over the head with the stipend thing!"

"Hold it", John continued. "When later in the evening he asked my opinion about the stipend stalemate, I told him many students and their families were facing a serious financial burden because of the elimination of the financial aid."

"You didn't even condemn the government!" Svend sneered. "You should have been much more forceful. Faced with a golden opportunity to stick it to our enemy number one, you were weak-kneed and chickened out. It's disgusting!"

"Come on, boys," John objected. "Do you really think a pleasant evening in a good atmosphere with an excellent dinner should be ruined by a pissing contest between me and the Prime Minister?"

They were upset with John's performance but calmed down when Erik chimed in.

"Fellows, don't jump on John. I think that under the circumstances, he handled the situation pretty well. Let's stop pointing fingers. The Bible says in Ephesians, and I quote, '*Do not let the sun go down while you are still angry and do not give the devil a foothold.*'"

"I agree," Svend said with a grin. "But the sun has not yet set, and the devil is the Prime Minister, and we are fighting hard to deny him a foothold!"

With a condescending air, Erik raised his voice. "Your understanding and interpretation of these sacred words are all screwed up!"

When the group resumed its deliberations about what to do next to keep up the pressure on the government, Peter said, "We're running out of parts on the bike. Now, only the gearwheel, frame, luggage rack and pedals are left. When these parts are gone, what do we do then?"

"Don't worry," Carl replied. "At the Opposition Leader's presentation the gearwheel will go. So, we still have enough parts for three more installments. If this is not sufficient, we'll think up something else. By the way, Erik, did the politician accept our invitation to appear? If so, I take it that you have made the practical arrangements!"

"Yes, everything is shipshape. He'll be on for number ten!"

"What about the broadcast after that?" John asked.

"So far our messages have been rather down-to-earth," Erik said. "I think it's time to throw into the mix something more lofty and literary. You've all heard about Emil Toft, last year's Poet Laureate. Maybe he would agree to participate in the eleventh segment. He's a prolific writer, and he could perhaps scribble down a profound poem and read it in support of our cause."

"Excellent suggestion! But, how can we contact him? Do you know where he lives, Erik?"

"I've heard he lives in the large hippie community called Freestate. Don't you guys remember that some years ago a couple of hundred hippies and homeless people took possession of an old abandoned and run-down apartment building and a surrounding area north of the city? Defying the authorities, they built several primitive clapboard cottages all over the place, set up their own sort of independent state with its own government, elections and laws. The authorities have tried on several occasions to evict them, but so far, these nuts have been able to resist being thrown out. It's a wild place—lots of drinking, sex and dope!"

"Well Erik," Svend said, "Since you came up with this brilliant idea, why don't you, being a literary type yourself, contact the scribe to sound him out?"

"That's okay with me. I'll take care of it," Erik agreed.

- - - -

The segment featuring the Leader of the Opposition, Willy Hansen, a social democrat, came on as planned. The group had decided it would be tactful not to appear on the program until after he had finished his presentation.

Willy Hansen faced the TV audience and began his speech:

"Good Evening. I'm here tonight as a member of the House of Representatives to express my views in the current debate surrounding the stipend matter. In the past, the student community has often stood shoulder to shoulder with my party and our labor unions in the battles to protect the workers and enhance their standard and quality of living.

"However, setting aside this mutually rewarding relationship, the stipend matter goes far beyond political ideology. It's purely a question of fairness and should not, *I repeat*, should not be political football. Our country prides itself in having one of the finest higher education systems in the world. It's based on the established, sound and fair principle that qualified candidates, regardless of their families' financial means, have absolutely free access to our institutions of higher learning.

"The government has, as you know, traditionally provided our students with financial support to help them cover their living expenses. However, it's a known fact that the administration has eliminated this much-needed stipend. As a nation, we have to ask ourselves: Do we not want these bright brains to concentrate all their time and efforts on their studies instead of being absent from the classrooms demonstrating? Do we want to see the quality and intensity of their education diluted by the need to cope with the cost of the bare necessities of life? The answer from my perspective is a resounding, No!

"We in the opposition have been working hard to pressure the administration to reinstate the crucial financial aid to our students, but so far in vain. However, we know that a couple of smaller parties in the current coalition government are starting to have second thoughts about the stipend matter. In addition, we will, within the next week or so, call for a vote on a motion to reverse this unfair edict. Unless the administration gives in, I am confident that we, along with some defectors in the coalition government, have enough votes to overrule the government. In that case, it will fall on a non-confidence vote, and under our Constitution, new elections will be held.

"To our nation's students let me say, keep up the demonstrations, but do it in a civilized and orderly manner. Unruly and violent behavior is not acceptable and will not help your cause. Thank you and good night."

When the politician left, the kidnappers emerged with the bicycle and dismantled the gearwheel.

Chapter 17

Erik approached the dilapidated six-story apartment building in the Freestate complex. It was located in a run-down area of the city. Its walls were covered with graffiti all the way up to the top floor. Two men in underwear, and without shoes, were sitting on empty beer crates inside the big, iron gate leading to the large open area behind the building. Empty beer and liquor bottles were strewn all over the area.

One of the men got up, approached the gate and asked. "What do you want?"

"I'd like to talk to Emil Toft, the poet. I understand he lives here."

"Yes, he normally lives in 6A, but he isn't always there. He sleeps around a lot, if you know what I mean."

"Where do you think he is now?"

"In our vegetable garden over there. He usually sits near the tomatoes. That oddball spends most of his time there jotting on scraps of paper. He's not very social unless he's drunk."

"Can you open the gate so I can get in?"

"Yes, if you swear you aren't on our shit-list of government dopes trying to throw us out!"

"I'm not," Erik swore.

With a beer bottle in hand, the fellow opened the heavy iron gate. Erik headed for the vegetable garden. Navigating through beds of lettuce, carrots, and beans, he eventually found a man sitting on the ground scribbling in deep concentration, surrounded by empty beer bottles and crumbled scraps of paper.

"Are you Emil Toft?" Erik asked.

Without looking up and continuing his writing the man muttered, "Yes, that's me."

"Mr. Toft . . ."

Before Erik could utter another word, the man held up his hairy arm and said, "Cut out that *mister* shit. My name is Emil!"

"Emil, I'm here to ask for your help."

"My help with what?"

Erik explained his group's mission. "Our program is known as the *Minister's Bicycle*. Haven't you seen it?"

"No! I've no television, and I don't want to watch anything on that dumb thing! It's a lot of garbage they show. People who watch that TV crap are brain-dead idiots! The main pillar in a civilized society should be the written word and not that junk!"

"I couldn't agree more, Emil. That's why I'm here. You see, we'd like to raise our arguments against the government to a higher level . . . like a literary one. You could assist us by appearing on our TV program with a poem and reading it."

"If it's knocking the goddamned government I'm ready. Those bastards have for months disturbed the peace in our community by trying to throw us out."

"Great, Emil, but we can't pay you for this."

"Don't worry about that. Just send me a case of beer when it's over."

"Thanks a lot, Emil. We'll pick you up next Wednesday at five-thirty. Is that okay with you?"

"Yes," he mumbled. "I'll be waiting outside the gate."

After Erik left, Emil took a big gulp of his beer, crumbled a scrap of paper and threw it into the tomato area.

Chapter 18

On the evening of the eleventh installment of the *Minister's Bicycle*, Emil was led into the make-up room at the NBS TV station.

Befuddled, he asked, "What the hell am I doing here?"

"Sir," replied the cosmetician, "We just want to fix you up a bit for your TV appearance, like combing your hair, and putting some make-up on your face."

"I don't want any of that stuff. What these numbskull viewers see is what they get. Instead, give me a couple of bottles of beer. I'm thirsty!"

A staffer brought him two cold beers, which he quickly downed. He wiped his mouth off on his sweater sleeve.

The TV anchorman appeared on TV with the following announcement:

"This evening's installment of the *Minister's Bicycle* will have a literary touch. We present to you, Emil Toft, last year's Poet Laureate."

Emil lumbered onto the stage. He wore old jeans, badly worn at the knees, a heavy wool sweater with holes and spots on it and flip-flops. His head was engulfed in a thick unkempt mane and a full shaggy beard covered most of his chest. He wiped off a pair of flexible wire-rimmed glasses on his sweater. He put on the glasses and intoned:

> *"Black clouds are sinking down on every learning room*
> *A dark age has come to fore in this Athena's land*
> *Her children flounder like leafless trees in the stormy night*
> *With lack of food for mouth and brain they cry*
> *Rise up - oh students and swing the mighty sword*
> *Defeat the beast – its bad will and void its evil sins*
> *Blood will flow but you must endure the fight*
> *Take heart the strangling rope will one day break*
> *Free at last – the cry will sound throughout the land*
> *Dawn has let the sunshine in – the food and brains are back."*

111

The poet took off his glasses and put them *and* the poem in his pocket.

Then suddenly, he turned toward the TV audience and said, "Since I'm here, I have a message for the nitwits in the government. Keep your sticky fingers off *Freestate*—the nation of free people to which I belong! We insist on our right to live peacefully without the harassment of you moronic bureaucrats! And to you sheepish viewers, sitting nailed night after night to the dumb TV set, let me say . . ."

Before Emil could utter another word, John, who had been sitting in the broadcast control room with the other kidnappers, rushed onto the stage and hauled him away out of the sight of the TV viewers.

After the poet was removed from the stage, the kidnappers appeared. Unfazed by the program glitch, Erik stood up and with a slight smile he said, "After these profound words by the pride of our nation, the Poet Laureate Emil Toft, we shall return to reality by removing the luggage rack. Now, Mr. Minister only the frame and pedals are left—enough for two more installments, and we'll be back. Good night, Sir!"

Chapter 19

Confident that he now had enough votes in support of his motion, Willy Hansen, the Leader of the opposition, asked the Speaker of the House to call a special session.

On that day, the *Gang of Five* joined hundreds of students in the packed spectator's gallery in the House. The Speaker rose from his chair at the elevated podium and read aloud the motion introduced by the opposition, and amid boisterous applause from the gallery, the proceedings began.

"Mr. Hansen," the Speaker boomed, "You may proceed."

Willy Hansen left the bench and mounted the lectern. "Mr. Speaker, for weeks, this House has been occupied by fruitless discussions concerning the stipend matter at the expense of other urgent legislation that requires action by this assembly. Therefore, Mr. Speaker, in an attempt to resolve, once and for all, the item on today's agenda, I have, on behalf of the opposition, placed before you and this House a motion to reinstate the financial aid to our university students. I, therefore, respectfully ask you, Mr. Speaker, to put our motion to a vote."

The speaker turned toward the Prime Minister who was sitting on the government bench and said, "Mr. Prime Minister, before we proceed with the vote on the motion placed before this House, have you anything to say in this matter?"

The Prime Minister rose and replied reluctantly, "Mr. Speaker, after extensive deliberations, my administration has decided to heed the call of the opposition to reinstate the stipend to the students attending our institutions of higher learning. Therefore, Mr. Speaker, I ask that the motion be withdrawn by the Leader of the Opposition."

Turning toward Willy Hansen, the Speaker asked, "Does the Leader agree to withdraw his motion?"

"Yes, Mr. Speaker, I do."

The Speaker continued. "Are there any objections to the Opposition Leader's answer?"

A resounding chorus of "No!" erupted in the spectator's gallery.

The Speaker, who had been munching on an apple throughout the proceedings, nearly choked while hammering the podium with his gavel and hollering in the direction of the gallery, "Order in the House!"

He waited a few minutes until the noise in the gallery had subsided and said, "Hearing no objections, this matter has been resolved by mutual consent, and the motion is hereby declared null and void by the Chair!"

Amid thunderous applause from the gallery, Willy Hansen left his bench and went over to the Prime Minister's seat, shook hands with him.

"Niels, we have fought many battles in this chamber," he said. "I am glad that, through our mutual agreement, this matter is now behind us. And, because we were able to agree, this resulted in a win-win solution for everyone involved! I thank you for your change of heart."

The Speaker, who had finished eating his apple, rose and with gavel in hand, declared, "There being no other business to come before this House, this session is hereby adjourned."

- - - -

The *Gang of Five* was ecstatic and rushed straight to their haunt to celebrate. In an atmosphere of exuberance, they exchanged wild high fives across the table upsetting several bottles of beer, which landed on the floor.

"Thank God, it's over," John said.

"I told you before. God works in mysterious ways," Erik added with a grin.

"Well fellows, we're no longer TV personalities. Now we have to go back to school. But, we have to conclude our appearances on television the right way. Any suggestions?"

"Yes," Peter said. "We've essentially dismantled the poor minister's bike. So, I would suggest we get him a new modern fancy two-wheeler, like a ten-speed Italian racing model. We could then go on TV again, without masks, with the new bike and make a nice speech to the minister. What about that?"

"Excellent idea!" John said. "But what are we going to do with his *old* bicycle?"

"He can, of course, have it back. But once he sees the Italian wonder of a bike, I don't think he'll ever ride the old one again!"

"All right boys. Erik you are the penman. Write the text of our final statement, and you, Peter, can deliver it in your usual lawyerlike manner."

- - - -

Before the last installment, the group met with Lars Petersen, Program Director of NBS to thank him for his cooperation.

"I'm happy for you that this stipend thing has been resolved," he said. "I'm glad I could be of help. However, all of us at NBS must now face the sad fact that our high TV ratings will, unfortunately, take a nosedive to the old level. Nevertheless, we have enjoyed the ride. And for us, it's a wake-up call. We must now review our program line-up to try to make it more appealing to our viewers." He added with a smile, "If you fellows have any ideas for future TV features, do not hesitate to let me know."

"Count on us, Lars," John said. "And we thank you for your willingness to stick out your neck for us. We meet regularly in Hviid's Wine Room for beer, and you have a standing invitation to be our guest for a round or two!"

- - - -

The following evening during the news broadcast the TV anchor said: "Tonight will be the last segment in the series, the *Minister's Bicycle*, and the kidnappers will now make their final statement."

The *Gang of Five* entered the stage—this time without masks—and held high a brand new Italian racing bike.

"Mr. Minister," Peter began, "We wish to express, on behalf of the entire university student community, our profound and heartfelt thanks to you for your never-failing and tireless efforts in reinstating the stipend. You have displayed an inordinately high level of statesmanship for which our nation can be justly proud.

"We realize that out of necessity, you've had to commute to and from your office by public transportation and we regret that. But, Mr. Minister, as you can see, we have bought this new bicycle for your mobile enjoyment and exercise. It's our gift to you for all you have done for our cause. We still have your old bicycle in our possession. It has been reassembled, serviced, and new tires have been put on. It has also been repainted. In short, it's now in excellent operating condition. We want to return it to you with our thanks for having borrowed it. With your new bicycle, you will now be able to alternate between two two-wheelers.

"Mr. Minister, with your permission we'll, at a mutually convenient time, pay you a visit at your home to hand over your new bicycle and review with you its many advanced features. You see, considerable innovations have taken place within the bicycle industry since you got your old bicycle. Also, your new bicycle can attain high speeds, which you may not be used to. Therefore, with your safety in mind, we'll provide you with a helmet as well.

In conclusion, allow us, Sir, to reiterate our deep gratitude for the bold action taken by you on behalf of this nation's university students. Good night, Sir."

Chapter 20

A visit to the minister's home was arranged, and the group arrived with the two bicycles. They were greeted by him and his wife in their garden. Svend explained the features of the new bike and handed the instruction manual and the helmet to the minister.

"Sir", John said, "We hope you will enjoy this wonder of a bicycle. You'll now be able to resume your daily exercise pedaling to and from your office. Do you want your old bicycle back?"

Gerda cut in and said, "Alex, I know you love your old bicycle, but you don't need two. You'll be much happier with this new one. I've told you before to get rid of that old thing!"

"But, Gerda, it looks like new now!"

"Forget it Alex, what's the point? We've no room for two. Why don't you let these fellows keep the old one? Consider it a trade-in."

"All right then. You guys can keep the old one," he said reluctantly.

"Mr. Minister," Erik said, "We'll keep it as a precious token of your keen interest in the welfare of our country's students."

"Well, boys," Gerda said, "Come inside for refreshments. You must be thirsty. We all need a drink after all the excitement."

After the students had left, the minister noticed a small, engraved plaque on the frame of his new bicycle. It read: *THANKS.*

- - - -

The students walked with the old bicycle to the railway station to catch a train back to the city. Suddenly, they saw the minister in sweat suit and helmet speeding down the road on his new bicycle.

"I see he's enjoying his new bike," John said. "But now, what are we going to do with his old one? Do any of you guys want it?"

"Hell no!" they replied.

"It's a paradox," Carl said. "We've been racking our brains to come up with new stuff for our TV appearances. Now we're stuck with this old thing and we can't even figure out what to do with it."

"Wait, when I think of it," Erik said, "I could use it. My own bike needs to be fixed."

- - - -

At the next regular get-together of the group, Erik arrived on the Minister's old bicycle and parked it along the outside wall of the café. His friends were already there.

"How was the ride on the minister's old bike?" Carl asked.

"Excellent. It runs like a dream but I forgot to lock it!"

"Don't worry about that! Let's have some beer."

When the waiter, Harry, approached their table to take their usual order, he exclaimed with surprise. "Wow! You are the fellows who came on TV with the *Minister's Bicycle* program. I recognized you when I saw you without masks during the last broadcast. I've been following this funny series each time it was shown. It was hilarious and I will miss it, now that it's over."

"So will we," Peter added. "It was quite a ride . . . no pun intended! Now we have to hit the damned books again—not too exciting."

"By the way," Harry continued, "Today, your first round of beer is on the house."

Fueled by a steady flow of beer the group spent the entire afternoon in high-spirited banter and laughter about their TV appearances.

"I think of all the shows we put on, the skit with the sickly student and the doctor was the best," Svend said. "Our poet friend's literary rambling was a clear runner-up, although he tried to screw up the program with his tirade at the government and his attempt to lecture the viewers. By the way, we have to remember to send the scribe a case of beer."

While the group continued their animated chatter, Harry walked around with a piece of paper in his hand showing it to guests at their tables. When he came to the group's table, he said, "The bicycle parked outside has been stolen and the thief left this note in the bar."

John took the note and read it aloud:

To Whom It May Concern. I've taken possession of the black bicycle parked outside. The rightful owner can claim it by dropping an envelope with 500 kroner in cash (no check) in Frederiksberg Park in the trash container nearest the toilet building. Be there at 10 o'clock tonight, and after the money has been dropped, the bicycle can be picked up at the north sidewall of the toilets.

The group bursts into laughter. "I'll be damned," Carl said, "That thing has been kidnapped again!" He turned toward the waiter and said, "Harry, it's not ours. It used to belong to the Minister of Education. We've had enough of that bike! Good riddance."

The waiter returned to the bar, crumbled the note and threw it in the wastepaper basket.

THE END

POETRY AND UNDERWEAR

Chapter 1

It was an early spring morning before sunrise. Chuck McIvern, his hair a mess, sat in his underwear in his small kitchen. He looked out into the street lined with old oak trees. He intensely watched squirrels dart back and forth across the street as they pursued each other up and down the tree trunks. The small, furry animals fascinated him. Each morning he silently watched the lively spectacle outside.

And, like any other morning, his old typewriter, sheets of paper, a worn and chewed pencil, and a half-empty beer bottle sat on the small table next to him.

Betty, with whom he lived, appeared in the kitchen doorway in a faded robe. Her hair was in curlers and she looked very sleepy.

"Are you sitting there watching the squirrels again?" she asked. "What's so special about them?"

Chuck took a gulp of his beer and replied, "I like to sit here at the window watching the show outside. It's like being in a circus with acrobats in constant motion.

"When I was a boy, my parents often took me to the traveling circuses when they were in town—I loved it. Now, I can sit in my *own* kitchen as a spectator. I can watch a spontaneous, unscripted, natural, and improvised circus performance. And it's all free—no box office, no throngs massing to get in, and no parking problems. In short . . . no hassle.

"It gives me a lot of inspiration to watch the squirrels' lifestyle throughout the year. In the fall, they rush around to find nuts and bury them within their own individual territories, which they mark off by peeing on the trees. This helps to keep other squirrels out. In late winter, they mate, and in the spring, they build their lofty nests.

"When I have finished this beer, I will write a poem in honor of these small, fascinating creatures, and I'll read it to you. What goes on in nature always stirs my feelings."

"You and your squirrels, poems, and feelings," Betty said sarcastically. "Are you not working today—I mean *real* work?"

"No, Dear, I'm not in the mood for that today. But writing is work *too*. To put down on paper the essence of one's feelings about a given situation or event is not easy, and it requires a lot of concentration and reflection to get the prose right."

"You're nuts! Why don't you get a steady job instead of the sporadic part-time work you get? When will your so-called inspiration wake you up to do something productive that brings home the dough? Our unpaid utility and telephone bills are piling up. We can hardly afford to put decent food on the table, and you just sit there, day in and day out, staring out the window. Have you no sense of responsibility? I clean three houses a day, and the pay is barely enough for us to get by. The most serious thing is that we are falling behind with the mortgage payments. Tell me, what do you intend to achieve with all that writing?"

"I'll tell you. When I have enough poems for a collection in book form, publishers will be falling over each other to get their fingers on my literary output. *Then*, our financial future will be secured. When the famous Frost and Whitman started out, I'm sure they faced money problems *too*. At first, no publishers were interested in Frost's work. So, he published his poems himself. Eventually, he *and* Whitman became well-respected and famous. Who knows, that could happen to me too."

"Chuck, that's a lot of naïve bullshit, and who are the two guys you are babbling about?"

"They were our country's most revered poets. Every word they wrote was packed with observations and emotions. Every line in their poems was like a breath of fresh air."

"Over the years, you've written enough poems to fill twenty libraries," she said. "What has been the result? We cannot wait for years hoping that you'll be famous one day. And, by the way, who wants to read that stuff? People want novels filled with action, mystery, and sex. Someone once told me a poet is a person suffering from *word diarrhea*."

Betty turned around, and as she headed for the bedroom to get dressed, Chuck got up, stopped her, and embraced her. He kissed her and said, "I love you Betty, and our love will always sustain us, even when the chips are down."

She returned his kiss and wriggled herself out of his embrace. "I have to hurry up getting dressed. I don't want to be late for work," she said.

Moments later, she was standing at the bus stop across the street waiting for the next bus.

Chapter 2

Charles "Chuck" McIvern and Betty Johnson had lived together for nearly fifteen years in a small, old, one and a half bedroom wooden house in a low-class area of Baltimore. The houses there were almost identical and dated back to the nineteenth century. They were originally built for workers in a large woodworking factory, which had closed down long ago. It now stood empty like a ruin—a lifeless and faded relic of past industrial activity in the sleepy and dilapidated neighborhood. Many of the houses were in ill repair—some abandoned, some had fallen to pieces, and others had burned down to the ground. Most of the tiny grounds in front and behind the houses were either barren, with only bits of grass and no flowers, or completely covered with tall weeds. Massive, centuries-old oak trees dominated the potholed street, their roots bulging through the sidewalks and their leaves overshadowing the dwellings.

Most of the inhabitants of the neighborhood were poor, unemployed, and retired people.

Chuck came from a wealthy family background. His grandfather had arrived in the United States from Scotland during the period of mass immigration. He started a small real estate business in Baltimore, building and leasing low-class dwellings to house migrant workers from Europe. Over the years, the enterprise grew and became very successful. It was expanded to include commercial real estate as well.

By the time Chuck's father took the helm of the family business, it had become a dominant player in the city's real estate market.

Chuck and his younger sister Elsie grew up in a large mansion in a fashionable area outside the city. The house was staffed with a cook, maid, nanny, driver, and a full-time gardener. Inside, the residence was exquisitely furnished with priceless antiques and paintings by old European masters.

Chuck and Elsie were enrolled in private schools. Chuck was a bright student who excelled in all academic subjects, but his main interest was literature. His essays always brought him an "A", and he graduated from high school with honors.

126

Both Chuck and Elsie were brought up under strong discipline, often taken to the extreme, especially by their father.

Chuck enjoyed much more freedom than Elsie did. Their parents were overly protective of her and placed considerable restrictions on her movements outside the home. She didn't have many friends, because first they had to be screened by her parents to determine whether they were appropriate acquaintances. Elsie often got into loud arguments with her parents, which ended with slamming of doors and her fleeing from the house, staying away for hours.

When Chuck was a teenager, his father often told him about the family's growing real estate business and its many new projects that were in the planning stages. Although he listened patiently, without enthusiasm, to his father's monologues, his mind was somewhere else. It was evident that his father hoped he would one day take over the family enterprise.

Whenever he sensed that his father wanted to bring up the matter, Chuck sought refuge under an old elm tree in the garden—either reading or writing. As a result, his relationship with his father became distant and formal.

When it was time for Chuck to enroll in college, he was granted a full scholarship at a prestigious institution. His father urged him to continue to graduate school and get an MBA, still hoping that Chuck would join the family enterprise. But, to his father's great disappointment, Chuck opted for a master's degree in Literature and Philosophy. He graduated *magna cum laude*.

At his graduation ceremony, the atmosphere between Chuck and his father was tense. Afterwards, when they were in the parking lot, his father had asked, "What are you going to do with your useless degrees? You won't be very employable!"

"Dad, I know," he answered. "But for me, real life is not to go to an office each day, rush around from nine to six in a rat race, and eventually end up with an ulcer or heart attack. And, I have absolutely *no* interest in the real estate business. I want to study life and write about it."

With an air of disdain, his father retorted, "How are you ever going to make a living by studying life and writing about it? What about getting stability and responsibility in your life?"

"Dad, don't worry about me. I'll get along fine. I'll find some work to do—something more interesting and productive than wearing a stiff shirt, and sitting in a wood-paneled office, in front of a computer with an overly perfumed private secretary at my fingertips."

"Well, don't come running to me when you're out of money!"

"Don't worry, Dad, I won't."

Since that conversation between Chuck and his father in the parking lot, they'd drifted further apart. From that point on, Chuck's only contact with his family was with his mother through occasional phone conversations. She managed to persuade her skeptical husband to provide Chuck with forty thousand dollars, which he used as down payment on a modest house.

Ultimately, Elsie dropped out of college. Her parents had hoped that she would marry a man with a business background who would join McIvern Realty and continue the family ownership tradition. Instead, she got involved with a group of hippies, and eventually left for Arizona to live in a commune there.

- - - -

Betty's early life was much different. Her parents were poor. Her father had been a part-time laborer moving from job to job without any stable income. Because of a severe drinking problem, he could rarely keep a job for long. He spent most of his time hanging around in a run-down public park. Often times, he would sit alone on a bench accompanied by a six-pack of beer and occasionally a half-empty vodka bottle. He would return home to their small apartment in the early evening—most of the time, drunk.

Betty witnessed loud arguments and outbursts of anger between her parents. This included verbal and physical abuse of her mother, who eventually suffered a series of nervous breakdowns, resulting in frequent stays in mental institutions. Whenever her mother was well enough, she did cleaning jobs. Betty often went along to help her with the heavy workload.

Because of the tumultuous scenes at home, her father's drunkenness and her mother's constant despair and depression, Betty hated staying in their small apartment and slipped away whenever possible. She spent time hanging around with other youths at a run-down basketball court in the neighborhood, which also happened to be a gathering place for teen-age drug dealers. She barely graduated from high school. A college education was out of the question because of her parents' dismal financial situation. Instead, when not assisting her mother, she worked as a waitress.

Chapter 3

The café where Chuck and Betty met had a history. Decades earlier a previous owner of the place, who faced bankruptcy, set fire to the café, hoping he could cash in on his insurance policy. Investigators determined that it was a case of arson, so the owner not only received nothing from the insurance company, he also landed in prison.

When the café was rebuilt, the new owner named it The Flame.

Patrons of The Flame were a blend of aspiring writers, vagrants, and groups of old men who met each morning for loud discussions. An odor of fried eggs, bacon and hash browns, mixed with aroma of coffee, filled the café.

When Chuck and Betty first saw each other there, they were in their early twenties. She had left home and was staying with friends. For weeks, they regularly met at The Flame, and over bottles of beer, Chuck read his poems to her. They took a liking to each other, fell in love, and eventually she moved in with him.

- - - -

During a phone conversation with his mother, Chuck told her about his relationship with Betty, and that she was his live-in companion. His mother was shocked.

"Who is that girl and what's she doing? Does she have a job?"

"She is a lovely girl, Mom. She comes from a poor screwed-up family, and right now she is cleaning houses." With a chuckle, he added, "I think she likes my poems."

An eerie silence followed. His mother sighed and asked, "Are you going to marry her?"

"No, Mom, that's not necessary. I love her very much, but we don't need a piece of paper to formalize our relationship and the love we feel for each other. Look, Mom, many marriages end in divorce, so what's the point of having a certificate that often turns out to be worthless? Think about all the anger and mudslinging—especially about money, following most breakups of marriages."

"But Chuck, what about starting a family?"

"It's not in the cards. Most people marry to have children. Should Betty and I decide later to start a family, we would, as a formality, do the paperwork. By the way, Betty feels the same way."

Chapter 4

For years, Chuck had spent most of his days sitting at the kitchen window in deep reflection, seeking inspiration for new poems and scribbling on his pad. When satisfied with the prose, he would transcribe them on his old typewriter. From time to time, these literary activities were, by sheer financial necessity, interrupted by part-time jobs. He had worked at building sites, mixing mortar, hauling bricks and drywall, and cleaning up the sites at the end of the day. He had worked for a trucking company delivering furniture, been a hotel elevator operator substitute, and a stock clerk in supermarkets and department stores.

Chuck liked to say that these sporadic, odd and low-paying jobs among what he called "real people," provided him with plenty of thoughts, inspiration, and fertile material for his poems.

As years passed, these jobs became less and less frequent, as he spent practically all his time writing. This increasingly became a point of irritation for Betty in her daily struggle to make ends meet.

- - - -

One evening when Betty had come home late, she slumped down from exhaustion on a kitchen chair. As usual, Chuck was sitting near the window with his writing materials and a bottle of beer. He got up and approached Betty, and kissed her.

"I've finished the poem *Nature's Circus*. Would you like to hear it?"

"Is it long?" she asked in a tired voice.

"No, it's a short one."

She sighed, and said in a muted voice, "Go ahead."

Downing the rest of his beer, Chuck grabbed a piece of paper, and standing in front of her, he intoned:

> *Daybreak has come and released me from Morpheus' arms*
> *I stagger through pots and pans to face the windowpane*
> *Through it, I see a world that wakes my sleepy limbs*
> *A street circus full of small acrobats sprinting around*

132

Instead of canvas and its poles a tent not made by man
A nature's canopy of leaves held up by massive trunks
No seats – no clowns – no horses, wild animals of any kind
But acrobats of nature's own delight my sleepy eyes
They dart up and down tent poles in happy frenzied play
Twist, turn, stop, and leap they do at dizzying speed
Like happy children, they play tag and hide-and-seek
High up below the roof they fly from pole to pole without a fright
There is no need for nets and ropes to catch a fateful fall
A daily show - it's free – no ticket, crowds and parking
With child-like eyes, I watch the show – I am in circus again

"Is that *all* you have been doing today—writing that poem?" Betty asked with a tinge of sarcasm in her voice.

"Yes Betty, but writing so the prose flows smoothly with rhythm is difficult. It requires a lot of concentration and editing. When I see the twists and turns of the squirrels out there, it's fertile material."

"I wish," she retorted, "you would have twisted and turned toward the kitchen sink full of dirty plates, pots and pans, rinsed them, and put them in the dishwasher! Let's talk about something else. I'm starving, but in no mood to cook tonight. What about a pizza? Here is a coupon for three dollars off a medium. Let's try the pizza place down the street next to Sam's convenience store. Get going!"

Chuck got up slowly from his chair. Noticing his hesitation, Betty asked, "What are you waiting for?"

"Betty, I am short of money today."

"What *else* is new?" she asked with a sigh. Then she handed him a ten-dollar bill. He put on his windbreaker and left the house.

- - - -

A short time later, Chuck returned with the pizza and they ate it in silence. After having finished the meal, they retired to the bedroom. When they were in bed, Chuck moved close to Betty and began fondling her. She pushed him away and muttered, "Not tonight, I've a headache."

Chuck sat up in bed. "Betty, your so-called headache reminds me of a story I heard the other day at The Flame. You want to hear it?"

133

"Yes, if it's not too long—I'm tired."

"Betty, it goes like this:

A married couple, Harry and Mary Lou, was in Africa as part of a safari group. While they were walking through the dense jungle, a male gorilla descended from a tree, grabbed Mary Lou and took her way up in a tree. Up there the gorilla began fondling her, and in desperation, she cried down to Harry.

"Harry! Harry! What shall I do? Help me!'

Looking up, Harry said, 'Tell him you have a headache!'"

Betty turned off the bedside lamp, turned her back to Chuck, and uttered, "Not funny. Good night."

- - - -

The next morning, when Chuck was looking out the window in deep thought, Betty appeared in the doorway to the kitchen. She was still groggy from sleep.

"We have to have a serious discussion," she mumbled.

"About what? Isn't it too early for a serious talk? I haven't had my morning beer yet!"

"No, it's not. We have to talk about money. It can't go on like this. We can't pay our bills. We are about to run out of money. Since your so-called inspiration to get work is for the dogs, and my modest income from cleaning is far from enough to get us through financially, we are in deep trouble. We're months behind with the mortgage payments, and I fear the bank will foreclose on the house. Our unpaid bills are piling up, and you are just *sitting* there daydreaming and scribbling. We have to do *something* to get out of this mess!"

Absentminded, and still looking out the window, Chuck asked, "Have you any suggestions?"

Irritated, Betty retorted, "Boy, you have the nerve to ask that question! You could get off your ass and get out there and get some work!"

"Betty dear, I *do* look for work, when I feel the situation is right."

She slumped down onto a chair in exasperation. "Bullshit!" she yelled. "I can tell you the situation is right—*right now*, unless you want to live in a cardboard box under some bridge!"

134

Chuck got up and approached her to kiss her. "Betty, you should know, despite our occasional money problems, we'll muddle through, and I love you."

She turned away to avoid his kiss. "*Occasional* you say?" she shouted. "You don't get it! You are a hopeless nut case!" She calmed down and continued. "If you really love me, get real and get some *work*. Well, I have to run now or I'll be late for work. *Someone* has to work, but tonight we have to continue our talk."

On her way out, Chuck kissed her. "That's okay with me."

- - - -

That evening, when Betty returned home from work, Chuck got up from his chair, embraced her and handed her a mug of steaming hot coffee.

"I have a temporary job lined up for next week."

She looked stunned. "What kind of work and for how long?"

"As a busboy at The Flame. When I was there today around noon, Carl, the owner, asked if I knew someone who could stand in for his busboy for two days next week. The kid has to have a wisdom tooth pulled. I told Carl that I could help him out."

Betty stared at him, shook her head, and sneered. "Hallelujah! For two days at the minimum wage! Could you not have found something better?"

"I couldn't very well say no to Carl, and perhaps I'll get some tips. By the way, how was your day, Betty?"

"It was so-so. Our shitty money situation was on my mind. My cleaning was sloppy. I think Adele, my customer, noticed that. Quite frankly, I'm getting tired of cleaning houses. I must find something else to do to bring home some decent money. Somebody told me I should consider entering the trunk show business."

"What's that?"

"It's where one makes arrangements with a supplier to sell its products in private homes to a group of invited people. The person who makes her house available usually gets a gift from the products on sale."

"What kind of stuff is sold at these private shows?"

"Many different things—mainly items of interest to women, like clothes, household items, cosmetics, and the like."

"What kind of products do you have in mind, Betty?"

"I'm thinking about ladies underwear. It's always in demand, and I'm sure by getting it direct from a supplier, it will be cheaper than what is sold in retail shops. And the shows take place in a home-like atmosphere, almost like a party, and the hostess usually provides refreshments for the invited guests."

"Why have you picked panties and bras instead of pots and pans?"

"They can be sexy products, and I want to find a supplier of daring lingerie. No woman, nowadays, wants to wear grandmother-style underwear. They want something exciting, small and alluring, which could perhaps create more intimacy at home. Many women, who are over the hill, or close to it, with sagging bodies and stale sex-lives, need to be propped up, so to speak, with fancy lingerie."

"I see your point, but tell me, where do you find the money to get started? Don't you have to pay for the stuff up front?"

"No, usually not. I'm told the merchandise is made available on consignment—meaning that one only pays for what has been sold. Although I don't know for sure, I believe that any unsold items can be returned."

"How do you make a profit?" Chuck asked.

"I'm not quite sure how it works. But, I assume I can add my profit to the purchase price *or* get a commission from the supplier on the suggested retail price. These details can be sorted out after I've found a supplier. But I need some money to buy some decent clothes, cosmetics, and jewelry. I need to look my best at the shows. I'd also need a van to transport the underwear."

"How would you get that?"

"Talk to the bank about getting a loan."

"A loan from the bank? I don't get it. You have told me we are up to our eyeballs in debt. Why don't you instead get a loan from the bank so we can get some decent food on the table?" he said with a grin.

"You're nuts. You don't understand the difference between starting a business and upgrading from pizza to sirloin steaks!"

"How do you find a supplier?"

"I don't know right now, but I'll check around."

Chapter 5

Betty had a very friendly relationship with Adele Wells, one of her cleaning customers. Whenever she was working in the house, they chatted a lot. One morning when Betty arrived, she noticed Adele's sullen mood.

"Adele, you look unhappy today. What's wrong?"

"It's that damned computer!"

"What do you mean?"

"I'll tell you, since my husband John got a computer, he has been in almost total seclusion—*Googling*."

"What's that?"

"Apparently, it's a computer program where one can dig out all sorts of information. When I ask him what he's doing, he says he's doing research."

"What is he researching?" Betty asked.

"Beats me! I've no idea. Every evening when he returns home from work, he hurries upstairs to his office and plays around with that dumb thing. When dinner is ready, I have to call him several times to come down and join the girls and me. Since he got that thing, he's been in another world.

"Very little conversation is going on now between him and me and the girls. Even when he comes down for breakfast in the morning, he fiddles with a small hand-held device and hardly finishes eating. When I ask him what he's doing, he tells me he is communicating with his computer upstairs.

"And, our sex-life is gone. Since he got his computer about six months ago we have only had sex three times, and each time I had to drag him along and do all the foreplay. He showed no interest. The whole thing was a dud and I've given up on sex with him."

"Adele, that's not normal."

"No! It's a disaster. Our family is coming apart. I've talked to some of my friends and several of them are facing the same problem. We have everything a family could wish for. John has a well-paying job, we have a wonderful house, and two adorable, bright daughters." Adele wiped off tears and continued. "If this continues much longer, I'm going to ask for a divorce."

"I hear you, Adele. Have you sat down with him and talked to him about the situation?"

"Yes, several times, but it's been a waste of time. He cannot see that anything is wrong. He says it's important for him to keep up-to-date with what's going on in the world by doing research to enrich his knowledge, but he's never specific."

"Have you talked to him about seeing a marriage counselor?"

"Yes I have. But he brushes it off as unnecessary."

When their conversation ended, Betty started cleaning, while Adele went upstairs to the bedroom, closed the blinds, and lay down on the bed.

Maybe John could do some research for me to find a supplier of lingerie, Betty thought. *But, I'll wait until I clean Adele's house next week to ask her if it's possible.*

- - - -

When she returned to Adele's house the following week, Betty said, "Adele, you will probably be fed up with me for suggesting this, but do you think John could do some research for me?"

Taken back, Adele asked, "What kind of research?"

"I would like to get a list of suppliers of ladies underwear."

"Ladies underwear? Why?" Adele asked, perplexed.

"I'm thinking about starting a trunk show business. You know what that is?"

"Sure, but does that mean you will stop cleaning?"

"Not completely. Don't worry, I will continue cleaning your house. You can count on that. But, if I decide to go ahead with this thing, do you think it would be possible to have a show in your house?"

"I'll think about that. As for the research," she added with a trace of sarcasm, "John would be ecstatic to do it."

"I understand, Adele, the computer crap is a sore point with you, but I absolutely have to find a supplier to get started with the business. My cleaning income is very modest and my financial situation is a mess. I'm living with a nut who, rather than working, is spending practically all his time writing poems—none of them may never be published. It's a serious problem."

"Although I'm reluctant to ask John," Adele said, "I'll do it for you."

On leaving the house, Betty hugged Adele and said, "Thank you. I hope I haven't added to your problem with John."

There was no reaction from Adele, as she opened the front door to let Betty out.

Chapter 6

In the evening when John returned home from work he went, as usual, straight upstairs to his computer. When dinner was ready, Adele called him to come down, and reluctantly he joined the family at the table. They ate in silence, and when they were ready for dessert, Adele said, "John, my cleaning woman, Betty, asked me today whether you could do some research for her."

His face lit up. "What does she want to know?"

"She needs a list of suppliers of ladies lingerie."

"No problem! I can easily do that."

Their daughters broke out in giggles, and one of them asked, "What does the cleaning woman need it for?"

"She plans to start a lingerie business," Adele answered.

When she brought in dessert, John got up.

"Are you not having dessert?" Adele asked.

"No, I'm already full. I have to get going with the research you asked me about."

He left the table and went upstairs, leaving Adele and the girls to eat their dessert alone. While clearing the table, Adele muttered, "Damned computer."

"It's hilarious—Dad researching underwear!" one of her daughters exclaimed.

- - - -

The next day Adele phoned Betty. "I have the list for you," she said tersely. "You can pick it up anytime."

The same afternoon Betty went to get the list. When she was about to leave, she said to Adele, "Thanks for the list. I hope I haven't ruined what is left of your relationship with John."

"Don't worry about that. It's already destroyed!"

"By the way," Betty added, "Could you write a favorable reference about me, just a few lines. But, don't mention the cleaning I do for you. Just write that we are friends and you vouch for my honesty, character, et cetera. You know what I mean."

"Sure, wait here a few minutes. I'll go upstairs and write it."

She returned with the note and Betty left the house.

Back home Betty joined Chuck in the kitchen. "I've got a list of suppliers of women's underwear from Adele," she said.

"How did she get it?" Chuck asked.

"Her husband found it on his computer."

"It's amazing the amount of information one can get on a computer," Chuck said. "I wouldn't mind getting one. Imagine the wealth of knowledge about poetry and literature I could dig out."

"You can forget about that, Chuck. Anyway, we can't afford to buy one." Mockingly, she continued, "You don't need one. You do enough research each day sitting there, near the window, getting all your so-called inspiration."

Betty sat down, poured herself a mug of coffee and began studying the list. It was comprehensive and detailed. For each supplier its brands were listed. She found one firm located in the outskirts of the city.

Then turning to Chuck, she said, "I found one supplier located in our area. The firm's name is *Elysee*. It sounds French and one of its brands is *Excitica*. No doubt, with names like that, it must be some daring stuff. What do you think, Chuck?"

"Sounds okay to me. Speaking of underwear, I hope you can sneak a set for yourself. Yours could use a bit of updating. You look your best without it. But be assured Betty, with or without your underwear, I love you dearly."

Chuck got up, took Betty in his arms, and kissed her. She wrestled herself free of his embrace, and said, "Every time I have a conversation with you, you turn it into a comedy."

Chapter 7

A couple of days later Betty phoned *Elysee* for an appointment. On the day of the meeting, she had put on her only decent outfit. She met with the owner, Linda Dare, in her office.

"What can I do for you, Mrs. Johnson?" Linda asked after their introduction.

"I've been thinking of starting a trunk show business in women's underwear. And I'm interested in one of your brands."

"You mean ladies lingerie," Linda corrected her. "Mrs. Johnson, do you have any retail sales experience? And what occupation do you have now?"

Betty hesitated for a moment, and then said, "I help people arrange the inside of their homes."

"I see. Like interior design work."

"Yes, something like that."

"Have you got any references? And what is the profession of your husband?"

Handing Linda Adele's note, she said, "He's an author."

Looking impressed, the owner said, "Mrs. Johnson, we carry several different labels. What kind of lingerie are you considering?"

"I was thinking of your *Excitica* line. It sounds exciting. Is it possible to have a look at that collection?"

"Certainly."

Betty was led into a small room, where Linda opened a box and put part of the *Excitica* collection on a table. She held up a set and said, "Isn't it adorable? It's a very exciting design. Don't you agree?"

"Yes, it's a perfect choice."

"Mrs. Johnson, before we get into the nitty-gritty of our relationship, let me give you a little background on my company. We are mainly a design firm, owned by my husband and me, and we have only a couple of employees. We are rather small and have been selling our lines to a few retail shops through a couple of local independent reps. The lines are manufactured by a local garment maker. We have a recommended retail price-list, but anyone dealing with us is free to set his or her own selling prices. However, we certainly don't want our products to be cheapened. As you know, price always contains an element of snobbism, especially when a product like lingerie is concerned."

"I absolutely agree. It has to be done in style, and I assure you I'll do the business in a classy manner," Betty said.

"Now, let me explain how our arrangement works. I'll make available to you, on consignment, a quantity of lingerie to be paid for as you sell it. However, since you don't pay me right away, I would need a bank guarantee from you that will remain in force for the duration of our business relationship. Is that acceptable to you?"

Hesitating for a moment, Betty replied, "I'm sure this can be arranged. I'll talk to my bank about it."

After the meeting, they shook hands, agreed to be on a first name basis and Betty left Linda's office and boarded a bus for the ride home.

- - - -

When she returned home and entered the kitchen, Chuck asked, "How did your meeting go?"

"Quite well, but I need two things—a loan and a bank guarantee."

"For what?"

"As I've said before, I need the money to buy a used van to transport the stuff and a couple of nice outfits including some decent shoes. I have nothing dressy—and also some cosmetics. I have to look presentable at the shows. The bank guarantee is required by *Elysee* since they give me a bunch of lingerie without payment up front."

"What *else* do you need?" Chuck grinned and added, "A facelift, perhaps?"

Betty slapped him playfully on the cheek. "Ha-ha, very funny!"

"I'm sorry, Dear, for getting out of line. You are the most beautiful woman in the world. You don't need it right now, but maybe down the road.

"So, tell me, Betty, how the heck do you think you can get all that from the bank? As far as I remember, the last bank statement showed a balance of something like one hundred and twenty dollars."

"We could use our house as security," Betty answered. "We have some equity in it, which should be more than enough to cover the loan and the bank guarantee."

"Hold it! You mean, *I* have equity in the house. Are you telling me I should gamble the roof over our heads for some underwear?"

"It's lingerie, and don't worry, it's not a gamble. If the business flops and I stop doing it, the lingerie can be returned and I don't have to pay anything."

"But we'll be stuck with the van!"

"Come on, Chuck. It's time that we got some wheels anyway. We have never owned a vehicle since we got together, and I'm tired of always having to take the bus. I'll phone the bank for an appointment, and I would like you to come along."

"Hell no! I've more productive things to do." He got up, kissed Betty on the cheek, and returned to his seat. "Good luck Dear, now that you and I, hopefully, will soon be in the money."

Shaking her head, Betty left the kitchen and Chuck resumed his writing.

Chapter 8

Betty arrived at the neighborhood branch of Community Bank and went straight to the office of Alex Hart, the manager. When she entered, he was sitting behind his desk munching on a hamburger. It was lunchtime. He got up, took a gulp of his Coke, and they exchanged introductions.

"What can I do for you today, Mrs. Johnson?" he asked.

"I need a loan and a bank guarantee."

"Do you have an account with us?"

"Yes, a joint account with Charles McIvern."

Alex Hart consulted his computer. "I found it. There has been very little activity on the account, and right now, it shows a balance of ninety-nine dollars and seventeen cents. Tell me, what do you need the loan and the bank guarantee for?"

"I intend to start a business."

"What kind of business?"

Betty told him the products were lingerie, explained how the business was done, and the purpose of the loan and the bank guarantee.

"Mrs. Johnson, do you have a formal written business plan, including the sales volume and the profit you expect to reach? You see, the credit committee at our head office needs this information to consider your application."

"No, Mr. Hart, I didn't think that was necessary. It's a small business, and I've no idea how much I can sell *or* the profit."

"I don't know whether our head office will waive this standard requirement. But tell me, how much cash would you need and the amount of the bank guarantee?"

"A loan for ten thousand and a bank guarantee for the same amount."

"Mrs. Johnson, could you give me specifics as to how you intend to spend the money?"

"I have to buy a second-hand van and some clothes."

"I see. What kind of security can you provide against the loan and the bank guarantee? I assume you own a house?"

145

"No, I don't own it. The owner is Charles McIvern. He has a mortgage with your bank."

"Who is he?"

"He's an author. I live with him."

Alex Hart checked his computer again. "Mrs. Johnson, Mr. McIvern's equity in his house is fifty thousand, eight hundred dollars, so, hopefully, there shouldn't be any problems. We would have to conduct a title search to determine that the property is free of any liens, but this is just a routine formality. Since he's the owner of the house, he would have to sign all the documentation. I'll submit the matter to our head office and let you know when I hear from them."

They shook hands, and Betty left the bank and headed for home.

When she appeared in the kitchen, Chuck asked, "Did you have a good meeting with the bank? Did you get the money and the bank guarantee?"

"Not yet. To get it, the bank needs *our* house as security. Then they have to get the approval of their head office. If they get it, you will have to sign all the papers since the house is in your name."

"So *I'll* be on the hook?" Chuck asked with a smile.

"Yes, I guess so."

"Betty, for you, the apple of my eye, I would gladly risk my fortune—everything I have, because I love you."

He got up from his chair, poured a mug of steaming hot coffee and handed it to Betty. "My Dear, drink this. Its warmth and aroma will relieve you of all the world's complexities and cares. They will fly away on eagles' wings."

With an ironic smile, she said, "Thank you for your kind words."

Chapter 9

A week later, Betty heard from the bank that the loan and the bank guarantee had been approved. She persuaded Chuck to accompany her to the bank and he signed the papers. Betty got the money and the bank guarantee.

Upon leaving the bank, Betty said, "Now we have to find a used car dealer so we can get the van."

"No problem," Chuck said. "Down at The Flame, I've met a nice guy named Pete. He's a salesman with A-One Pre-Owned Cars. I suggest we go there and talk to him."

When they arrived at the dealership, Chuck recognized Pete at the end of the dusty gravel lot. "Hi, Pete!" he yelled.

Puffing, the pudgy salesman came running toward them. He was dressed in an old-fashioned, faded light-blue suit with pointed shoulders and over-sized lapels. A large flame-red bowtie and a pair of worn cowboy boots completed his attire. He caught his breath and wiped sweat off his forehead.

"What's new Chuck?" he asked. "I didn't see you down at The Flame this week." Without waiting for an answer, he continued, "What can I do for you and your pretty lady?"

"We are here to look for a used van."

"You mean a pre-owned one? We have one over there. It's a '99 Dodge—in mint condition. Come, let me show it to you."

After passing a long row of used vehicles, they arrived at the van. It was covered with dirt. Its original blue color had almost disappeared, the front bumper was badly dented and one windshield wiper was missing.

"Come on Pete, is that what you guys call *mint condition?*" Chuck asked.

"It just needs a few things fixed," Pete replied, "But wait until you see the inside." He tried to open the door on the driver's side. It was stuck and he couldn't open it. "It's a bit tight," he said. "A little grease will do the trick."

He went around to the passenger side and opened the door. "Come take a look. It's in beautiful condition inside."

Betty and Chuck looked inside and noticed a tear in one of the seats. They shook their heads. "Inside it looks a little better than outside, but it won't do," Betty said.

Pete banged the door shut and the front bumper fell off.

"What kind of shit are you trying to sell us?" Chuck asked.

"But, Chuck, at one thousand, five hundred, it's a steal. But, if you want to step up in price, I have a beauty down there at the end of the lot. It's a Ford van, 2001 model, in super condition. Only one hundred and twenty thousand miles on the baby—one owner—all highway miles. The guy was a traveling salesman peddling multi-grain bread all over the state."

They walked down to the van, and on inspection, Betty found it to be in decent condition, and asked. "How much is this one?"

"Three thousand, five hundred."

"Too high for our budget," Betty said. "What about three thousand?"

Pete squirmed, and hesitating for a moment, he said, "Okay, for you *only*."

"We'll take it," Betty said.

"Do you guys want financing? We have a fantastic plan—only one percent over prime."

"No, we'll pay cash," Betty replied.

They followed Pete to the business office to complete the paperwork. It was a small cinderblock building. Inside, it was dirty and messy. Old papers and vehicle parts were strewn all over. Two cats walked around as if they owned the place, and a distinct smell of cat food and a cat litter box filled the small office. The owner of the dealership was fast asleep at a small desk in the corner of the room with a cat resting in his lap.

"Let's sit down over there at the conference table," Pete said.

The conference table was a small plastic one, covered with old newspapers, dirty paper cups and plates, plus a couple of empty root beer cans. They sat down, and when Chuck was about to sign the sales contract, one of the cats jumped up on the table. It walked around on top of the contract with its tail high and stopped with its rear end close to Chuck's face.

When he pushed it away, Pete kicked his leg, and frowning he whispered, "Don't do that, it's the boss' favorite cat."

Fortunately, the owner, who was still fast asleep, did not notice the incident. When they left the office, Pete said, "Phew! That was a close call. If the owner had seen what you did to his favorite cat, I'm sure the deal would have been off."

"Damned cat," Chuck said. "It stuck its ass right up in my face!"

When they sat down in the van, Betty handed Chuck the key and said, "You're the driver. Let's get going!"

"Not me! My license expired years ago," he mumbled. "What about yours?"

Betty checked her purse and found her license. She turned the ignition but the van wouldn't start. She looked at the fuel gauge—no gas.

Chuck stepped out of the van and yelled, "Pete, there is no gas in this thing!"

"Chuck, I'm coming!"

Pete arrived with an old rusty gas can, poured some gas in the tank and said, "It's on the house!"

- - - -

On their way home, they stopped to fill up. As Betty had not driven for years, parking at the curb in front of the house became a difficult maneuver. After several tries, and with the help of Chuck standing outside, she eventually got the van within a couple of feet from the curb.

Chapter 10

With the bank formalities completed, Betty phoned Linda Dare for an appointment. Not fully comfortable driving in the city, she left the van at home, and boarded a bus for the trip to *Elysee*. When she met Linda, she handed her the bank guarantee. Linda looked at it, puzzled.

"The guarantee is issued on behalf of a Charles McIvern. Who is he?"

"I live with him," Betty answered.

"I see, but since he is the applicant mentioned in the document, I believe that my business relationship is with him, and not you. Let me call my lawyer."

She phoned her attorney, and after a brief conversation with him, she said. "Mr. McIvern will have to sign the agreement for the sale of the products since legally I'm doing business with him. Also, I need a simple letter from him authorizing you to do the business on his behalf. This is just a formality."

Betty left Linda's office and headed home. When she entered the kitchen, Chuck got up from his chair, greeted her with a kiss, and asked, "Is everything wrapped up?"

"Almost, but Linda told me you'll have to sign the contract with her since your name is in the documents. She also needs a letter from you authorizing me to do the business on your behalf."

When Betty put the contract on the table in front of Chuck, he glanced at it with disdain and said, "I don't want to read that legal crap. It's been written by a bunch of lawyers in language nobody can understand. It's a prostitution of the English language. It lacks clarity, and the syntax is horrible. But for you, Dear, I'll sign it."

"What about the letter?" she asked.

"You can write it yourself, and I'll sign it. If you need help in writing it, the dictionary is over there on the shelf." Then he added, with self-aggrandizing humor, "Betty, I'm a poet. I cannot stoop down from my lofty literary pedestal to write that kind of simple letter, but if you want it in verse form, I'm, of course, prepared to write it."

"You are crazy!" Betty retorted. She sat down, wrote the letter, and Chuck signed it.

- - - -

The next day Betty returned to the office of *Elysee* and handed Linda the signed sales agreement and the letter of authorization. To get Betty started it was agreed that Linda would, based on her statistics of the most popular color and sizes, prepare a suitable assortment of lingerie.

With all the formalities behind her, Betty's thoughts for the next several days centered on where to launch the business.

Maybe Adele would be willing to make her home available for the first show, she thought.

She phoned Adele and said, "You will recall that I asked you a few weeks ago whether it would be possible to have a show in your house. Would you agree to host the first event in your home? If so, you probably know a lot of women who might be interested in attending."

"Yes, Betty. As I've already told you, there's not much excitement in my home, so I think it would be a nice distraction for me. And it's true, I know several women belonging to my church, and I have a list of members from our country club. I'll spread the word and write a few notes to my closest friends."

"Thank you, Adele, I really appreciate you help."

"Is there anything else I can do, Betty?" Adele asked.

"Yes, if you could have coffee, soft drinks and cookies available for the show, it would be great. Of course, I'll reimburse you for the expenses. All the items in the collection are daring and sexy, and as a gift, you can pick a couple of sets for yourself."

Chapter 11

On the day of the event, Betty arrived at Adele's house with her van full of cartons containing lingerie. She wore a pink décolletage-style dress that was cut low in front and back, stiletto shoes, and layers of costume jewelry dangling around her neck and wrists. Her hair had been dyed blond and supplemented by a hairpiece for fullness. A liberal amount of rouge and mascara accentuated her facial features.

Adele helped Betty lay out the lingerie in neat rows on the dining room table, extended by leaves, and on a couple of small tables in the adjacent living room. Two coffee makers were in full production, and a selection of other refreshments and cookies was put out.

The collection was varied. The pieces came in sizes from small to extra large—most of them, perhaps understandably, in the latter size. For needed stability and fullness, several bras were padded. Some items were of simple designs, while others were decorated with laces. Colors from traditional white and beige to black and pink created a symphony of shades.

The women arrived in a steady stream, and it wasn't long before the dining room and the living room were filled to capacity. The ladies, like the lingerie, came in all sizes. Some of them, no doubt, believed the acquisition of the items displayed would perhaps have a beneficial effect on their bodies and private lives and contribute to increased excitement, intimacy, and harmony at home.

Betty mounted a stool and addressed the crowd. "Ladies, Adele and I welcome you to this show. My name is Betty Johnson. I'm an independent distributor for the exciting *Excitica* line of lingerie you see in front of you. The sizes and shapes of the garments have been designed anatomically to fit a variety of women. I'm sure you will find the pieces *uplifting!* Take your time to browse through the collection, and if you have any questions or need any advice, I would be delighted to assist you. At this time, I'm not yet ready to accept credit card payments—only cash or checks. Thanks again for coming."

Stepping down from the stool, Betty tripped in her unfamiliar stilettos and landed on the floor. Unfazed, she got up quickly, corrected her hairpiece that was out of place, composed herself, and said, "And now, Adele will say a few words."

Adele got up on the stool and announced, "If any of you ladies would like to try out the lingerie you are more than welcome to use the guest bathroom on this floor or any of the two bathrooms upstairs. You can use the garage or the small tool shed in the garden as well. Also, I invite you to refresh yourselves with coffee or sodas and the home-baked cookies over there. Please make yourselves at home."

The assembled women eagerly threw themselves over the displayed garments, and anxious fingers traveled feverishly through the neatly arranged rows of lingerie. It was an animated scene, and it didn't take long before the orderly rows turned into a jumble. Sales were brisk and the restroom facilities had continuous heavy traffic to the detriment of those ladies having pressing natural needs.

Several women ventured out to the garage to try out their choices. The place was teeming with activity and the women, who had made their choices, formed a long line to pay for their purchases.

A heavyset woman, whose dimensions, both vertical and horizontal, were rather large, entered the guest toilet. Her wide wingspan enabled her to carry a large selection of lingerie with her into the sanctuary. After having locked the door, she hurriedly began trying on her potential choices. As it took quite a long time for her to go through the large amount of lingerie and pick the right sets, a few ladies outside banged impatiently on the door eager for their turn.

The woman inside feverishly sped up her process. She had placed several pieces in the sink and others on a small table. They landed on the floor after she had tried them on, and a bra fell into the toilet bowl. Rather than trying to pick it up the wet garment, she became embarrassed, lost her marbles and flushed. To her horror, the bra got stuck inside the toilet, which started to overflow, wetting the floor and soaking the lingerie strewn all over it.

She opened the door and screamed, "There's something terribly wrong with the commode. It's overflowing!"

Adele rushed into the toilet. She was in shock when she saw the wet mess on the floor. She grabbed the telephone and called a plumber, who informed her he would be there within fifteen minutes.

Meanwhile, most of the lingerie had been sold, and the women, who had focused their full attention on the lingerie and ignored the refreshments, started to leave—including the hefty one, who despite the toilet predicament, had finally managed to pick a set for herself.

- - - -

A short time later, the plumber arrived. Upon entering the dining room, the few remaining pieces of lingerie caught his attention.

"Is that stuff for sale?" he asked.

Wearily, Adele answered, "Yes."

"It's my wife's birthday tomorrow," he said. "I think she would like a new bra as a gift."

"What size does she wear?" Betty asked. "And what color do you think she would like?"

"She's kind of big—I believe an extra-large would do the trick—and black looks exciting."

Betty picked out the bra, wrapped it in paper, and after the plumber had paid, he carefully put it in his tool bag and entered the bathroom. After having fixed the problem, he emerged. Holding high the wet bra, he said, "Wow, you must have had quite a party here! This thing got stuck in your toilet!" Then he picked up his tool bag and left.

When alone, after all the women had left, Betty and Adele, exhausted from the bustle of activity, slumped down into a sofa.

"Thank God, it's over, Betty said. "Apart from the toilet mishap and the soaked lingerie, I think the show was a huge success. Don't you agree, Adele?"

"Yes! The plumber got a present for his wife because of a clogged toilet—it's all too funny!" Adele laughed.

"Did you pick a couple of sets for yourself?" Betty asked.

"Yes I did, a turquoise and a pink one."

Betty smiled and said, "I hope your new lingerie will be successful competing with the computer for John's attention."

"Don't bank on it. It would take a miracle to get his ass away from that thing! Anyway, the event was a lot of fun. But, tell me, what are you going to do with the wet pieces?"

"No problem. I'll wash and iron them. They will be as good as new," Betty answered.

They began cleaning up the place and Betty asked, "Adele, how much do I owe you for the refreshments and the plumber?"

"Don't worry about that. I had a fun time. Excitement in this house is in short supply, and the toilet needed a check-up anyway."

Upon leaving the house, Betty said, "Adele, thanks a lot for hosting my first show. The next cleaning of your home is on me."

They embraced, and in a happy mood, Betty drove home quickly. She was anxious to share with Chuck the successful outcome of her first venture into the business world.

Chapter 12

Chuck was waiting for her in the kitchen. "How did the show work out?" he asked.

"It was incredible," she said. "I sold almost the entire assortment and made nearly three thousand dollars. Despite a stuffed toilet and some wet underwear, the show was a solid success."

With an air of puzzlement, Chuck asked, "What was the problem with a malfunctioning john and the wet underwear?"

When he heard Betty's explanation, he quipped, "You see the perils of doing business? Commercial activity is a minefield. That's why I rejected my dad's invitation to join his business."

"Now," Betty said, "we can take care of some of the unpaid bills and one of the three mortgage payments still outstanding."

"And I can get a computer. My old Underwood that I've had since college is too slow and cumbersome to capture my soaring thoughts—and it has no spell-check."

"Chuck, as long as I stay in *this* house you're not getting a computer. I know from Adele how that thing can destroy the harmony in a relationship. Because of her husband's total preoccupation with that dumb thing their marriage is coming apart!"

"Betty, believe me, that would never happen to us. My deep love for you would never be the slightest bit affected, even by ten computers—never!"

"You're not getting a computer! I'll have more shows, and when I've brought our financial situation under full control, you can get a new electronic typewriter—period!"

Chuck got up, took Betty in his arms, and whispered in her ear, "You are *too* kind—I love you."

- - - -

As a result of the success of the first show, Betty was bombarded with requests from several women who were present at the first event to arrange similar private sales in their homes. Over the following months, her business was booming. The money flowed in so fast that it didn't take long before the outstanding mortgage payments and all unpaid bills were settled. She even paid off the bank loan and there was still money left over. Except for Adele's house, she stopped cleaning. Chuck's ration of three beers a day was increased to four.

The news of the trunk shows had spread like a bushfire all over the city and its suburbs. Soon Betty realized she couldn't handle the activities alone. She hired two women to help her cope with the expanding business. After having instructed them what to do, she let them loose. She junked the old van and got two new ones. She had them painted pink, and on the sides, *Lingerie on Wheels* was affixed in bold white letters.

- - - -

One evening when Betty returned home after a hectic day, she said to Chuck, "I never dreamed that a thing as simple as a trunk show could stir up that much interest and excitement. But I have to find some new ways to increase the business. Have you any suggestions, Chuck?"

"You're asking the wrong person. You know I have no interest in business, and my knowledge and understanding of it is near zilch. Businesses do, of course, advertise to create interest for their products. Another thing some companies do to promote their business and enhance their sometimes flawed reputation, is to donate money to charities and other good causes, to show what good and caring corporate citizens they are. In most cases they do this primarily to reduce or avoid paying taxes rather than showing genuine generosity toward the charities."

"Chuck, you gave me an idea! What about contacting some charities to find out whether they might be interested in sponsoring my trunk shows, and in turn, I will donate to them a percentage of my sales? I can afford that because of the big quantity discounts I get from *Elysee*."

"It's a good idea," he said. "It's always a laudable thing to give back to society a part of what one has taken from gullible people in the first place." With a wry grin, he added, "You could ask Adele if her husband could do some research to dig out a list of charities and other good causes."

157

"You must be kidding!" Betty retorted. "That's out of the question! It's a sore point with her. Anyway, we already know of several charities and associations that need to raise money for their activities. Let's try to make up a list ourselves."

They sat down at the kitchen table and began writing down as many names they could think of. The list included The United Way, The Red Cross, The Salvation Army, Goodwill, ASPCA, YMCA, The Historical Society, Boy Scouts, churches and many more.

"We can eliminate most of the big ones. They will probably feel they are too prominent and high-brow to get involved," Betty said.

"You are right. To associate the Salvation Army with the sale of sexy underwear is a doubtful proposition. Goodwill is another no-no. They are mainly interested in raising money by reselling used clothes, including perhaps, pre-owned underwear.

"The YMCA may be a potential candidate if you had a line of sports bras for their health-nut members, although many of them probably don't wear bras. As for the Historical Society, which buys and preserves historical landmarks, the promotion of 'Bras for Bricks' is another non-starter. Churches may be a possibility, although they may have a problem relating the sale of sexy bras and panties to their preaching of the gospel and their aim to lead their flocks to ultimate salvation. Why don't you ask some of your past cleaning customers if they have any suggestions?"

"When I think of it, one of my former customers, Louise Cook, enthusiastically told me about a large evangelical church to which she belongs. She supports it with money, and she said the church was always aggressively trying to raise funds for its activities. I'll give her a ring."

Betty dialed Louise's number. "Hello, Louise, Betty here. How are you doing?"

"Hi Betty! I'm doing fine. Although, I'm disappointed that you have stopped cleaning for me. I've tried several women but none of them clean as well and thoroughly as you."

"I'm sorry about that, but I was frankly getting tired of cleaning and the money was not there. Now I'm doing trunk shows, selling lingerie *and* doing very well."

"I know, Betty. I've heard about your shows through friends of mine."

"The reason I'm calling you is that you told me some time ago about your church and its interest in raising money."

"Yes, it's true, they need money. Most of the congregation pays a tithe to the church, but it's always interested in new sources of donations for its various projects."

"What's a tithe?"

"It's ten percent of a family's income. It's required to give that, according to the Bible."

"Do you think, Louise, that your church would be interested in sponsoring a sale of my lingerie to raise money. I would donate to your church part of my profit on the sales."

"I see no reason why my church wouldn't welcome that. It's a good idea. If you are interested in finding out what's going on there, I suggest you join me for the next Wednesday evening service. Would you like to do that? You could come to my place and we can leave together."

"Sure, I would love that. And I look forward to seeing you again."

Betty hung up the phone and turned toward Chuck. "I'm attending church with Louise next Wednesday evening."

"What! Is that a new thing?" He asked. "I didn't know you had an interest in religion. Does this mean you intend to attend church regularly?"

"Oh no, not at all, but Louise thinks her church might be interested in a trunk show to raise money. She asked me to come along for the evening service to get an idea of how big the church is. By attending I can get a profile of its members, like average ages, how they are dressed, their level of enthusiasm, and other traits—like some sort of market research."

"Betty, what's going on? You talk like a damned business person!"

"Hasn't it dawned on you that I *am* a damned business person?" She cocked her head and disappeared into the living room.

Chapter 13

Louise's non-denominational church, Mount Zion Ministries, was started by Jack Ross about ten years ago.

Pastor Jack, as he was called by his adoring and devoted flock, was a handsome and charismatic single man in his late thirties. Before founding his church, he had been the lead singer and guitarist of a small hard-rock band. For years, they had been playing in small joints in the city, with occasional gigs around the state. On the road, they spent the nights in cheap motels, and their ragged lives involved heavy drinking, drugs, and one-night stands with groupies. They never recorded anything and barely covered their traveling and living expenses.

Pastor Jack struggled with this lifestyle and, as he later told his congregation, he had a revelation from God directing him to start a church. From modest beginnings, in rented storefronts, his congregation grew larger and larger. Eventually heavy donations from his growing flock and a bank loan enabled him to build a large modern edifice to house his congregation, which had grown to nearly three thousand souls.

The exterior and interior of the church were modern. It resembled more a concert hall than a place of worship. No altar or other religious symbols were present, except for a huge white cross in the background of the stage.

Louise and Betty arrived at the church early to get a good seat. People were streaming in. The crowd consisted mainly of young adults and middle age people. Only a few elderly persons were in attendance.

The service began with loud Christian rock music from a band backed up by swaying background singers. The church went dark, and all of a sudden, Pastor Jack appeared in a glaring spotlight. To the blasts of the band, he leaped onto the stage.

"How are you all doing today?" he yelled. "Has God blessed you today?"

The congregation hollered back in unison that they were, indeed, well and blessed.

Dressed impeccably in a dark suit, white shirt, and colorful necktie, Pastor Jack moved briskly around on the stage during the sermon whipping up a frenzy among his faithful—often shouting in *tongues*. His topic for the evening was "The Gospel of Prosperity".

"Accumulation of riches and possessions," he intoned, "is perfectly acceptable to God, and when some of it is given to God through *this* church, it will come back multiplied."

The congregation responded enthusiastically to the sermon by stretching their arms high, closing their eyes, while some mumbled in tongues. Pastor Jack concluded the service with a thundering, *"Praise the Lord!"*

When Betty and Louise were outside, Louise asked, "Wasn't it inspiring? Did you like the service?"

"Yes, it was quite an experience." With a grin, Betty added. "I hope the congregation will show as much enthusiasm for my lingerie as they do for Pastor Jack's sermon."

"I think so," Louise said. "I bet you a trunk show in this church will be a success."

"Well then, Louise. Our next step is to meet with Pastor Jack. Do you think you can arrange that?"

"Sure, I'll take care of that."

- - - -

When Betty arrived home, Chuck asked her, "Did you enjoy the service?" He smiled broadly and added, "Did you get saved?"

"Not really, but it *was* interesting. The crowd was huge—mainly young and middle-aged folks. Very few elderly people were there. The church had a band that played rock-style Christian music—not the kind you hear in traditional churches."

"I'm not surprised. Young people stay away from traditional churches, which are, generally speaking, rather dogmatic and stodgy. They want something *hip*, and when that kind of music is thrown in, they get all excited. And most of these evangelical preachers are smooth-talking and charismatic types, able to hypnotize their followers."

"So, what did *you* do tonight?" Betty asked Chuck, changing the subject.

161

"I went down to The Flame, where I met Pete and the other guys."

"How many beers did you have?"

"I think only two."

"Shame on you!" she said sternly. "You already had three before I left for church, and that makes it one over your limit!"

In a huff, she left the kitchen, while Chuck turned his attention to his typewriter.

Chapter 14

Louise and Betty met with Pastor Jack in his office. When they entered, he was sitting behind an old, ornately painted desk. He got up and greeted them.

"Please have a seat," he said to the two women.

"Pastor Jack," Betty started. "I admire your beautiful desk."

"Yes, it's nice. It's a French Renaissance piece—a gift from an antique dealer. He *was* homosexual, but through my intercession, God saved him from his sinful life-style and he became normal again. He's now an avid member of my congregation."

He changed the direction of the conversation and asked, "What can I do for you ladies?"

"We are here," Louise began, "to talk to you about a possible fund-raising project for our church."

Pastor Jack's face lit up. "Great, but first let's bow our heads and ask for God's blessing on our conversation."

He seized the hands of Betty and Louise from across the desk. Closing his eyes, he began to pray. When finished, he said, "Okay, shoot!"

"I understand," Louise said, "that our church needs funds for its expansion, and my friend here, Betty Johnson, has a fund-raising idea. I'll let her explain what's involved."

Betty outlined the plan and told Pastor Jack she would donate twenty percent of the sales to his church, and that she would handle refreshments for the event.

"It sounds very exciting," he said. "We could have the show in connection with a service right after the end of this month—when people get their paychecks. Would that be convenient for you, Mrs. Johnson?"

"Yes, no problem."

"All right then. I'll make the announcement at the next service."

Betty and Louise got up, shook hands with the pastor and left.

- - - -

A few days later, after the service, Pastor Jack addressed the congregation.

"Your tithing is vitally important to cover the expenses of our church, and I'm grateful for your generosity. However, as you know, we have several outreach programs including plans to open a preschool, so that at an early age, our small ones can receive a solid Christian foundation that will serve them well throughout their lives.

"Our church needs additional money to fund these projects. To raise these funds, following this month's last service, we will have a lingerie sale. A well-known supplier of women's apparel will be present with a large and varied collection of lingerie. She has offered to donate a sizeable percentage of the sales to our church.

"The lingerie is fashionable and daring, which I'm sure will excite our women and, dare I say, the men in our congregation as well. Some of you may question why a Christian church like ours should get involved in the sale of this kind of underwear. Isn't that idolatry of the flesh as opposed to spiritual nourishment of the soul? Not so! Anything that may contribute to increased excitement and intimacy is perfectly acceptable to God. The Holy Book contains many references to this. *Proverbs,* Chapter 5, and *Songs of Solomon,* Chapters 7 and 8, are good examples. Therefore, I trust all of you women will turn up in force to buy the lingerie, and thereby help your church financially to carry out its mission, as demanded by God."

Chapter 15

Chuck's communication with his mother had been infrequent over the years. Whenever they were in contact by phone, it was evident from the tenor of their conversations that the absence of a close relationship pained both of them.

One day she phoned Chuck. "As I have already told you, your father has been in very poor health for the last couple of years. He decided some time ago to sell the business to a national real estate group. Your father has suffered a series of strokes and is now in a wheelchair. His health and his mind are failing day by day. For far too many years, you've had *no* contact with him. Now that he is nearing the end of his life, I think you should come and visit him. I would be grateful to you if you did, and I know your father would appreciate it too."

"Yes, Mom. I'll come over tomorrow. Is that convenient for you and Dad?"

"Certainly! We would be delighted to see you again."

The next day Chuck arrived at his parent's home. Before entering, he stood still for a moment in deep thought. He reminisced about his childhood there. He reflected on the beauty of the residence and the large garden with its floral symphony of colors. He recognized the trees, which had grown huge with majestic canopies of leaves casting large shadows over the house. He saw the old elm tree, once his favorite climbing spot and the place where his early fumbling attempts to write poetry began. He walked around in the garden, unconsciously tracing his childhood footprints. The memories of things past overwhelmed him, and his eyes became moist.

He approached the massive front door and rang the bell. A maid opened the door, and as he entered the large hall with its white and black checkered marble floor, his mother appeared and hurried toward him and embraced him.

"Chuck, how are you doing my boy?" she asked.

"I'm doing fine, Mom. What about you?"

"I'm all right, although age has slowed me down and I worry about Dad. Come, let's join him in the library."

They entered the library. Chuck's father was sitting in a wheelchair reading. The *Wall Street Journal* obscured his face.

"Charles, look who is here!" she said.

He slowly lowered the paper into his lap. He looked frail and thin, and with an air of mild surprise in his sunken face, he muttered, "Is it you Chuck?"

"Yes Dad, it's me."

"What brings you here? I haven't seen you since you graduated with those worthless degrees."

Ignoring his father's remarks about his education, Chuck answered, "I just wanted to stop by to say hello to you and Mom. I'm sorry that you are not feeling well."

Coughing heavily, his father feebly uttered, "Yes, I'm feeling weak. Not exciting to spend day in and day out in this damned wheelchair unable to do anything productive."

"I understand, Dad. I hope you will soon feel better."

"By the way," his father continued, "What are you doing these days? Are you still living with that woman? What's her name?"

"Yes. Her name is Betty. She is now a successful businesswoman, and I'm still writing poems."

"Have you had anything published?"

"Not yet, Dad, but when my collection is large enough, I intend to try to have it published."

"There is no money in writing poems. I told you that years ago. And what is this Betty selling?"

"She is selling lingerie."

Chuck's mother, who had been sitting still listening to their conversation, got up and asked, "How about some refreshments? What would you like, Chuck?"

"A beer, please."

"What about me?" his father asked.

"Charles, you can't have any alcohol—doctor's orders. You can have a soft drink.

He shook his head and resumed his reading.

Chuck got his beer and his mother had a glass of white wine. They drank in silence. When Chuck had finished his beer, he got up and said, "Well, Mom and Dad, it's time for me to leave."

He went over to the wheelchair to say good-bye to his father who took his outstretched hand and held it tight. Chuck felt a slight pressure of his father's hand in his, and tears welled up in his eyes. His father let go of his hand. Chuck bent down and kissed him on the forehead.

He stood still for a moment in front of his father who looked up and said, "Take good care of yourself, my boy."

With that, Chuck left the library followed by his mother. Once they were out in the hall, she said, "Thank you, Chuck, for stopping by. You made me *and* your dad very happy."

"I'm glad I came, Mom. Stay well and take good care of Dad."

He kissed his mother. She held him tight, as if she didn't want him to leave. Finally, she let him go of him. He walked slowly down to the gate. Out in the street he turned around to take one more look at the house. Then he went to the nearest bus stop to catch a ride home.

Chapter 16

Betty and Louise spent most of the day preparing for the lingerie sale in the church after the evening service. They unloaded cartons of lingerie, crates of soft drinks, and boxes of cookies from Betty's van and carried it all into a large assembly room adjacent to the sanctuary. The lingerie was laid out on long tables in neat rows by size and color.

When the service was over, Pastor Jack addressed the congregation. "The lingerie fund-raiser will now take place in our assembly hall. Although this event is primarily of interest to our women, you men are, of course, welcome to attend the show as well."

Then he added with a grin, "You men may be able to help your ladies select some exciting pieces." Amid laughter from the congregation, he continued. "But, you men are free to leave, although I would suggest that those of you who are not joining the ladies remain seated and we'll have a bible study. After I give a short introduction to get the sale started, I'll be back so we can begin studying the Holy Scriptures."

Pastor Jack went to the assembly hall followed by a throng of women. When the room was filled to capacity, he mounted a podium and prayed.

"Almighty God, we ask you to bless this event, and we pray for a successful outcome, enabling this church to carry out its mission in your name."

With closed eyes and mumbling in tongues, he stretched out his hand towards the underwear as a sign of blessing and said, "Amen."

After Pastor Jack had left, Betty mounted the podium.

"A hearty welcome to all you ladies . . . *and* men. My name is Betty Johnson. I represent the *Excitica* collection of lingerie you see on these tables. It's the latest and most modern designs—excellent quality and durability, *and* easily washable. Take your time and browse through the collection. Louise and I are standing by ready to assist you if you have any questions or need advice as to what to pick. If any of you need to try on the pieces, I understand there are four ladies restrooms, and if that's not enough to handle the traffic, you can use the men's restrooms as well."

Most of the women were excited about the displayed lingerie, and their eager manipulation of the pieces quickly turned the orderly rows into a mess of colors and sizes.

Other women were more discreet, and approached the selection with considerably more dignity. The show lasted well into the evening and was a solid success. When it was over, Betty made a tally of the sales and handed Pastor Jack a check for the twenty percent of the take.

"Thank you, Pastor Jack, for allowing me to have the event in your church. Here's a gift for you," Betty said. She handed him a box with a red ribbon around it. "Since underwear was involved, I didn't want you to be left out!" she said slyly.

- - - -

When Betty arrived home, she enthusiastically gave Chuck an account of the show.

"It was a great success. Pastor Jack was happy with the check I gave him, and I presented him with a gift—a nice set of men's underwear."

"Very fitting," Chuck commented with a laugh. "A very practical present for the good pastor. I'm sure it made his day. By the way, I had a successful day too. As you will recall, a few days ago, I submitted a poem, entitled *Tired Hands*, to the metal workers union, and they agreed to publish it in their next newsletter."

"Did they pay you anything for that?"

"No! They don't have much money lying around. The recent strike by their members nearly emptied their coffers. But it's a great honor to have a poem featured in such a prestigious publication, and it shows there's a receptive market for good poetry."

"Yeah! As long as it is free-of-charge," she scoffed.

Chapter 17

A few weeks after Chuck's visit to his parents, his father died. The memorial service took place in the Episcopal Church they attended every Sunday. It was filled to capacity by relatives, friends, and business connections of the deceased. Before the sermon, the President of the city's Chamber of Commerce gave a short speech praising the many virtues of Charles McIvern Sr., with complimentary remarks about his generosity toward a host of charities.

After the service, the funeral cortege proceeded to the cemetery for the interment at the family plot. During the brief graveside ceremony, one could hear in the distance the mournful sound of bagpipes.

When the funeral was over, Betty turned toward Chuck's mother, whom she had never met before, and said, "Mrs. McIvern, my condolences to you, for the sad loss of your husband."

"Thank you, Betty. It was nice of you to come. I'll have some people over to my house for refreshments, and I would like you both to join us."

The three of them walked in silence to the waiting limousine. After a short stay at the residence, the driver dropped off Betty and Chuck at their house.

- - - -

One evening, weeks later, Chuck and Betty were sitting in the kitchen. She was writing checks to pay bills and he was hammering away on his typewriter. All of a sudden, he stopped.

"By the way," he said. "While you were out peddling underwear, the bank phoned to tell me that ten million dollars had been deposited in our bank account. It's probably an advance on my inheritance from my dad."

"Wow, what a surprise!" Betty exclaimed. "We're capitalists now!"

"Don't get carried away! We are *not* capitalists and *never* will be. That money fell in my lap—it was purely a windfall. I didn't do anything to get it. I don't know how my father amassed his great wealth. Was it entirely through honest dealings or did someone along the way get screwed? Most money is tainted, and we really don't need much to get along. However, if it could be put to worthwhile use to off-set any likely inequities and greed that may have led to its accumulation, then it has some value."

"What's that lofty talk supposed to mean?" Betty asked. "Are you going to give the money away?"

"Most of it, yes! But I have to get a computer first. It will make my writing easier and it has spell check."

"You know my feelings about computers," she said.

"I know, but don't worry. No computer will in any way impair our relationship and affect the deep love I feel for you. Now let's have some coffee."

Chapter 18

Chuck had built up a large collection of poems, which he entitled *Thoughts in a Chimney*, and decided it was time to try to get them published. With the help of his newly acquired computer, he was able to get a list of publishers. He wrote to several of them with enclosed copies of some of his poems. Some ignored his letters and others sent pre-printed rejection letters. Finally, he gave up.

"No publishers are interested in my collection of poems," he said to Betty. "I can't believe there's no interest in poetry anymore. I guess most readers, now-a-days, want salivating family dramas, and you know why? Because they can relate them to their own screwed-up family situations. Novels loaded with juicy sex are also in high demand because of the readers' own stale sex lives. Mysteries create excitement for humdrum lives. Most of those who read this so-called literature are desperately seeking to enter a fantasy world to escape from their own tedious ones.

"Deep thoughts and reflections on real life, as expressed in good poetry, don't sell. Our society is undergoing a total cultural degeneration. On top of all this, TV, misuse of computers, and all that other electronic crap are erasing the need for the written word."

"Chuck, have you finished your speech?" Betty asked.

"No, Dear, there's more to come, but for today, it's enough!"

"By the way, why do you call the poems, 'Thoughts in a Chimney'? Sounds like an odd title."

"Because, my Dear, the soul is like the fire inside a burning wood stove. Thoughts are rising from the soul like hot air and smoke is soaring through the chimney."

Laughing, Betty said, "Then, wouldn't it be better to change the title to 'Hot Air in a Chimney'?"

"Very funny," Chuck replied. "By the way, what's your opinion about the poems I've already read to you?"

"I find them somewhat complicated and difficult to understand."

"I'm not surprised. Your reading and comprehension is limited to the label texts on underwear!"

After this episode of literary dueling, Betty served Chuck a mug of coffee and asked, "Chuck, since no one wants to publish your poems, what are you going to do with all that paper?"

"I'll publish the collection myself—like Frost had to do, when he started out."

"Come on, Chuck, how are you going to do that, and who will read *that* stuff?"

"Simple! I'll find a printing firm, and the cost of printing will be a drop in the bucket thanks to my dear, late, father. And I will give away the books free-of-charge."

"But what about promotion and distribution?" she asked skeptically.

"Again, very simple, my Dear. The Flame will be my promotion and distribution center. I'll sit at a table signing the books, and anyone who comes in will get a signed copy, free-of-charge. I'll run a couple of small ads in our major daily newspaper. There will be a large sign outside The Flame inviting people in. I expect large crowds, and Carl, the owner of the place, will be doing brisk business in hamburgers, hotdogs, hash browns, and other delicacies of the house. It's going to be quite an event."

"You're nuts. It's a waste of money!"

"Betty, what's money, anyway? When we started out, we had practically no money. Yet, we muddled along, and the love we felt and *still* feel for each other is the strong glue that blissfully binds us together, whether we have money or not. Money is just paper printed in Washington in amounts the government thinks is needed. It's no constant. It goes up and down in value. And, apart from meeting the bare necessities of life, its sole purpose is to entice people to buy things they don't need."

"Chuck, every time we have a conversation, you turn your comments into poetic and philosophical rants. Your understanding of money and its role in the economy is all screwed up. Money is the life blood of economic activity."

"You're wrong, my Dear. Money is the life blood of greed!"

That was the end of their discussion. Chuck returned to his writing, while Betty started preparing their dinner.

Chapter 19

Chuck had his collection of poems printed. The cover of the book, showing a chimney billowing smoke, was designed by an artist friend of his and a regular at The Flame.

The following announcement appeared in the city's major daily paper:

The public is invited to attend the signing and free distribution of Charles
McIvern's collection of poems,
"Thoughts in a Chimney"
Date: May 17 from dawn to dusk.
Venue: The Flame Café

- - - -

Early in the morning on the day of the event, Betty and Chuck arrived at the café with their van full of cartons of books, unloaded them, and stacked them inside. A large sign outside invited people to come in.

It wasn't long before a crowd from all walks of life descended upon the café. A long line of people formed out into the street. They were young and old, men and women. Workers in stained over-alls, hippies, vagrants, and sprinkles of professional men in coat and tie turned up. Even chimneysweepers were there, as evidenced by a couple of vans from Clean Sweep and Soot Doctor parked in the street. They were presumably intrigued by the title of the book, perhaps, hoping to get some hints benefiting their profession. The literary critic of the major daily also turned up.

Chuck sat at a small table with a bottle of beer within reach. Betty sat next to him handing him the books as fast as he could sign them. The books were snapped up at a rapid clip. The café's kitchen was overwhelmed with orders. The event lasted well into the evening, and at ten o'clock, an exhausted Carl announced that he was closing the place. That did not sit well with those in the crowd who were still waiting to get their books.

Fearing a riotous scene, Chuck stood up and announced. "For those of you who haven't got your copy yet, don't worry. We'll continue the signing and distribution tomorrow."

Slowly the throng dispersed into the street, and when all of them had left, Carl locked the entrance door and slumped down on a chair.

"Why did you tell them to come back tomorrow?" he asked. "I can't take another day of mob scenes. Me and my guys in the kitchen ran out of gas. We are completely exhausted, and it will take days for us to recuperate from this chaos."

"Come on, Carl, just one more day, and it will be over. And for you, as owner of this joint, it must be a financial bonanza. And don't forget, I'm a good customer here."

"Okay, Chuck, but for *one* more day only!"

Chuck and Betty left, and when they were back home, Chuck said, "As I expected, the event was a huge success. It clearly shows there is a keen interest in poetry. It encourages me to keep on writing."

"How naïve you are," Betty remarked. "Of course, it was a hit because they got the damned books *free-of-charge*. Do you really believe reading your philosophical mish-mash will revolutionize the interest in poetry? I doubt that!"

Chuck got up from his chair, kissed Betty and said, "It's late. We are both tired, let's go to bed."

- - - -

When Chuck and Betty arrived the following morning, they noticed that Carl looked depressed.

"What's wrong?" Chuck asked. "You look weary!"

"My hamburger guy called in sick this morning. He can't come to work today. He has tennis elbow."

"I didn't know the fellow played tennis!"

"He got it from flipping hamburgers. I'm now short-staffed and I don't know if I can handle another mob of invaders!"

"Don't worry," Betty injected. "I can take his place."

She went around the counter, put on an apron, and started the grill.

The news of the previous day's signing event had spread all over the city, and an even larger crowd than the day before turned up. Late in the evening, when Carl wanted to close down the place, several people refused to leave. Only after he had shut off all the lights did the holdovers reluctantly leave.

"Thank God, this thing is over," Carl said when they were alone. "My place is a mess now and I ran out of hash browns and toilet paper! I'm getting too old to run this joint. I hope I'll one day find someone to take it over."

Most of the books had been given away. After having helped Carl and his waitress clean up the café, Betty and Chuck returned home.

- - - -

A few days later the literary critic, who had picked up a book at The Flame, wrote the following review in the paper:

"Poetry in this land has, for far too long, been in a state of hibernation with only a few poems worth reading, seeing the light of day. Out of this literary wilderness, a new poet has emerged. Charles McIvern's recently published collection of poems entitled 'Thoughts in a Chimney' is a breath of fresh air. With a firm unwavering pen, he deals with a host of life's peculiarities and idiosyncrasies, tackling a wide spectrum of ordinary life situations. His poem 'Tired Hands' is a vividly painted picture of the travails of the underprivileged and disenfranchised in our society. Underlying his thoughtful reflections are discernible tinges of humor that makes one smile. His prose is wonderfully sparse and flows in a smooth cadence, void of unnecessary embellishments. His poetry places him right up there with our nation's most revered masters and, in my opinion, he should be a candidate for 'Poet Laureate of the Year'. I can heartily recommend 'Thoughts in a Chimney'. Its probing observations of human life provide us with a wealth of rich and soaring material to stir our souls."

The review caught the attention of a publishing house. It acquired the rights to the collection, which was re-issued for nationwide distribution. A series of book-signing events at the major bookseller chains were being suggested to Chuck, which he turned down.

Chapter 20

A few months later, Betty decided to get out of the trunk show business, and she handed over the activity to the women she had hired earlier. They also got the vans. Still interested in staying active in her trade, she leased space downtown and set up a boutique selling luxury lingerie.

Chuck bought The Flame and changed its name to Café Poetica. It quickly became a favorite haunt for both established and budding poets. They met there regularly for literary discussions. Once a week a poet would read a poem followed by critique by his or her assembled peers.

- - - -

One late evening, when Betty and Chuck were sitting in the kitchen, she said, "Our financial situation is now very sound, and I think we should get out of this shabby neighborhood and move into a bigger and nicer house in a better area. We can afford that. What do you think of that, Chuck?"

"No way, Betty, we should remain here. This is where our relationship began. It was here we struggled for years to make ends meet. These memories are precious. It is near the old café where we met and fell in love. Our new wealth should not go to our heads. But, if you would like to make this place neater—like repainting the house inside, getting a new bathroom, new furniture, and new appliances—it's okay with me. We could arrange a small vegetable garden behind the house, so we could be self-sufficient in the healthy stuff. We should, of course, also get a small hybrid car with high gas mileage."

"It's ridiculous to remain here for sentimental reasons!" Betty retorted.

Chuck took a beer out of the refrigerator. "Our roots are here, *period!* And it's here that I get inspiration to write!" After taking a gulp of his beer, he continued. "By the way, we got a pizza coupon in the mail—five dollars off a large. What about celebrating the good news we have had lately with a thick and chewy pizza loaded with pepperoni, cheese, and mushrooms?"

This practical proposal ended the discussion. Chuck put on his windbreaker and headed for the pizza place down the street.

When he returned, Betty had set the table with her best tablecloth, and decorated it with two lit candles and a small flower arrangement in the middle. They sat down and ate the pizza in silence. When the meal was over, Chuck got up, went around the table. He bent down, kissed Betty, and said, "This was a delicious and romantic dinner!"

Chapter 21

It was a wintry morning just after daybreak. Chuck was sitting in his underwear at his usual spot, near the window in the kitchen, with his computer and a bottle of beer. He was in a happy mood as he watched the squirrels' frantic romantic play in the trees outside. His intense observations were interrupted when Betty entered, elegantly dressed for work. She went over to him, kissed him, and poured herself a mug of coffee.

"I'm leaving early today," she said. "A new shipment of lingerie is in and has to be put on the shelves before I open."

Chuck followed Betty to the front door and opened it for her. When she was out on the front steps, she stopped and turned towards him and said, "I hate to bring it up again, but I can't stand living in this shabby neighborhood any longer. We have to move. I have a nice boutique downtown with high-class lingerie and we live in this dump. It doesn't make sense."

"Betty, Dear, as much as I would do anything for you, moving away is a *no*. If we were to relocate to another area, who knows, there may not be any squirrels there!"

"You're *nuts!*" Betty exclaimed, leaving the house in a huff.

THE END

THANK YOU FOR READING
POETRY AND UNDEWEAR
AND OTHER STORIES

WWW.OLEGIESE.COM

- *Post an online review*
- *Write a review on your blog*
- *Tell your family and friends*

181

30065477R00115

Made in the USA
Charleston, SC
03 June 2014